Prophet Muhammad as the Exalted Ruler of Arabian Peninsula

Prophet Muhammad as the Exalted Ruler of Arabian Peninsula

Habibur Rehman

ATLANTIC
PUBLISHERS & DISTRIBUTORS (P) LTD

Published by
ATLANTIC
PUBLISHERS & DISTRIBUTORS (P) LTD
7/22, Ansari Road, Darya Ganj,
New Delhi-110002
Phones : +91-11-40775252, 23273880, 23275880, 23280451
Fax : +91-11-23285873
Web : www.atlanticbooks.com
E-mail : orders@atlanticbooks.com

Branch Office
5, Nallathambi Street, Wallajah Road,
Chennai-600002
Phones : +91-44-64611085, 32413319
E-mail : chennai@atlanticbooks.com

Printed in India at Nice Printing Press, A-33/3A, Site-IV,
Industrial Area, Sahibabad, Ghaziabad, U.P.

Preface

For forty years the people of Makkah pronounced Holy Prophet of Islam as "most trustworthy" and "most honest." However, when he invited them for the worship of one true God in the capacity of the Messenger of God, they became blood-thirsty. They persecuted him, harassed his family members and tortured his followers for thirteen long years; but despite facing unprecedented agonies neither he moved from his mission nor his pious companions deviated from their straight path. When the Quraish of Makkah decided to liquidate him, he moved from Makkah to Medina to avoid bloodshed. There also they did not allow him to live in peace. They mounted attacks upon him at Medina one after another but were badly humiliated and defeated. Within ten years he became the undisputed Ruler of Arabian Peninsula.

I am fully conscious of the fact that innumerable intellectuals, thinkers, theologians and philosophers have done awe-inspiring, thought-provoking and wonderful work on the multi-dimensional aspects of the Holy Prophet. I, however, felt that many geniuses and wise men advertently or inadvertently perhaps thought it better not to magnify his contribution as the Ruler of Islamic Kingdom as much as they did in other cases. Historical records testify to this fact that he fought many wars and battles as the Ruler and the Commander-in-Chief of Islamic forces, and entered into alliances with several tribes, groups and clans as the Sovereign Power of Medina. He wrote letters to emperors, kings, monarchs and the rulers as the Chief of Islamic State and met envoys of various countries, nationalities and kingdoms as the Head of Arabian Peninsula, and governed people as the Steward of Mankind. The world around him too considered him as the grand Emperor of the region. I have tried to restate in a humble way what others have expressed wisely, intelligently and aptly in their own ways about the Prophet as the Ruler of Islamic State.

It is the fact in history that the Prophet never declared himself as the emperor, king, monarch or Ruler of Islamic Kingdom because he was not at all interested in worldly charms. He had rejected such offers when the Sardars of Quraish had approached him. He fought no war to capture any land, attacked no country to usurp any territory, started no battle to subdue any nation, and marched upon no kingdom to control any segment of people. It were his adversaries who attacked him one after the other and got defeated at his hands that made him the undisputed Ruler of Arabia. He projected himself only as the Messenger of God which was his highest status among the people of the world. History shows us that many people became emperors, monarchs, kings and rulers by their efforts but none became the Messenger of God save by the Mercy of the Lord. However, when God bestowed upon him the kingdom, he proved to be the unique, rarest, unmatchable and exemplary ruler.

The Prophet did not put any glamorous crown, never occupied any magnificent throne, did not live among splendid forts and fortresses, never enjoyed the charms of majestic mansions and palaces, never wore gemmed and jewelled robes, and never kept the army of servants and helpers. He governed from the mudded floor of the Mosque, passed his life in his thatched apartments made up of stones and adobe bricks, wore a simple and dignified dress and moved alone among people without any bodyguard. Mostly he ate dates and barley bread, and many a time fire did not burn in his house; he had to sleep hungry due to paucity of burning fuels. He sat on a mat supported by a leather pillow stuffed with fibers along with his water pot near his feet and a few clothes hung on the wall. He mended his dress, stitched his shoes and did household chores by himself. When the Prophet left this world his august body was shrouded in three white sahooli cotton clothes which had neither head cloth nor casing.

Despite being the Exalted Ruler of a magnificent kingdom he voluntarily set for himself sublime and superhuman aim which was never set before by any emperor on any part of the globe. Human records reveal that no man on earth ever undertook a task so far beyond human power with such feeble means as he did. Apparently, he had no other power except himself and no other aid save a handful of companions living in the remotest part of the desert; but he brought about such a huge and lasting revolution which was not accomplished before by any other human being. He neither founded dynasties, nor established kingdoms nor spread empires as the most famous men did, but with greatness of purpose, smallness of means and astonishing results he moved the altars, changed belief systems, abolished false gods, shattered armies, influenced legislations, impacted the governing structures, and changed the hearts of millions of people living in the inhabited world. The Prophet united people of every tongue and race, taught them wisdom, purified their hearts, gave them a code of conduct and made them enlightened human beings. In less than two centuries after his demise his followers reigned over whole of Arabia and conquered Persia, Egypt, Transoxania, Abyssinia, North Africa, Western India, Spain, and part of Gulf as well as numerous Islands of Mediterranean Sea. He was indeed the greatest by all standards by which human greatness may be measured.

Habibur Rehman

Acknowledgements

I am immensely grateful to all eminent personalities whose contributions, suggestions and assistance helped me to undertake this work. I am also thankful to my wife Mrs. Masarrat Habib, daughter Dr. Sitwat Khan, son Eng. Bilal Habib, son-in-law Dr. Jamshedur Rehman Khan, daughter-in-law Dr. Reshma Mukhtar, grandson-in-law Dr. Danish Kazmi, grandson Eng. Basil Habib Khan, and granddaughters Dr. Areeba Kazmi Khan, Eng. Abeer Khan, Ms. Rahma Habib Khan and Ms. Rifa Habib Khan; and all other well-wishers who helped me in giving shape to this venture.

Habibur Rehman

Contents

1

The Birth of a Unique Personality on the Earth

At the very outset the author would like to remind his learned readers that he had endeavored to undertake such a task which was more perplexing, astonishing and hypnotizing than Einstein's theory of Relativity which emphasized that if someone traveled in space in a vehicle with speed more than the velocity of light today, he would return on earth in yesterday. People were puzzled after hearing the claim of the scientist because they could not digest the idea that by travelling with the speed faster than the velocity of light one could return in yesterday which had already gone in obscurity. The author too is highlighting a more strange, mind-boggling and bewildering truth by saying that once upon a time there ruled an Exalted Ruler on earth whose empire was one of the biggest in the world and who was known throughout the world for his grace, benevolence and majesty but he was extremely poor, highly indigent and utterly penniless. He had set for himself voluntarily the troublesome ways of living of the ordinary people which were not set by any monarch on earth. He undertook the task of governing people through simple and feeble means which was not done before. He had ample resources and the army of the committed companions but with greatness of purpose, firmness of faith and his exemplary conduct he accomplished the huge and lasting revolution which was never achieved by any human being on the globe. He moved nations, territories and kingdoms, subdued emperors, kings, monarchs and rulers, altered legislations, social institutions and governing practices, impacted belief systems, ideas, ideologies and won the hearts of the people living in the inhabited world. It was due to his inspiration that a small army of inspired soldiers embarked upon one of the most thrilling victories in human history. They rapidly conquered Mesopotamia, Syria, Palestine, Egypt, North Africa, Gibraltar and Spain and carved out one of the largest empire the world had ever seen extending from India to Atlantic Ocean.

One would be astonished to know that the same Ruler did not use his kingdom's money for his personal use. He mostly ate barley breads, very often slept hungry due to lack of food, stitched his own clothes, mended the shoes, brought household material from the market, lived in a bricked house covered with palm leaves, had no bodyguard and when he died he left nothing for his heir. The author is hundred percent certain that it will be difficult for the people to believe in his above contention because Emperorship and its grace, grandeur and excellence are incompatible with hunger, poverty, meekness and physical and material constraints. For instance, nobody would believe if someone says that the Emperor of Japan Akihito washes his own clothes and does his work himself or the Queen of England Elizabeth does not own any property save some household utensils or Mukesh Ambani has only a thatched house whose roofs leak during rainy season or fire does not lit in the house of Bill Gates for weeks as he mostly sleeps hungry. People know that if someone is an Emperor, Queen, business magnate or a rich and a famous individual he or she would surely, certainly and necessarily live a luxurious, lofty and fantastic life and his or her behaviour pattern too would be generally egocentric, splendid, exalted and glamorous. It rarely happens in the history of mankind when people face a truth which is stranger than fiction. The author is highlighting that rare among the rarest truth by saying that such a unique personality was none other than Muhammad (PBUH)—The Exalted Ruler of Arabian Peninsula who was most humble among the humblest, extremely simple among the simplest, highly meek among the meekest as well as unpretentious, modest and unassuming. Despite being magnificent, noble and sublime he lived like a mediocre, commoner and an ordinary person but changed the tone and temper of civilizations and the map of the world by his genius and wisdom. When one writes about such a mightiest, glorious and brilliant person, one is bound to suffocate due to paucity of appropriate words, proper sentences, suitable similes, befitting adjectives and apt connotations. The author too had to starve because he could not find suitable superlatives and appropriate analogies, semblances, similitude and analogies to highlight the majesty and magnanimity of the merciful Ruler. Moreover, the style that he had to adopt to explain his contribution and impact upon mankind too felt short due to non-availability of befitting letters, vowels and consonants in human dictionary. It is hoped that the enlightened readers would forgive him and bear with him for not doing justice to the unique and the exemplary Ruler the world had ever seen.

THE SOVEREIGNTY AND THE SUPREMACY OF THE LORD PRIOR TO THE CREATED WORLD

A moment has passed in the pre-universe period, when there was neither time nor space nor consciousness nor matter nor energy nor motion nor force. There was neither existence nor non-existence nor life nor death nor vacuum nor void. No sign was there, neither the days' nor the night's divider nor the bloom of dawn nor the gloom of dusk nor the glimpse of light nor the thickness of darkness. The charms of elixir were shapeless, the manifestations of creation were formless and the silence of death was faceless. There was no realm of heavens and earth, no territories of suns and moons, no kingdoms of stars and galaxies, no domain of air and water, no zone of clouds and sky and nothing beyond that. The odd and even were not born, the mortals and immortals were conspicuous by absence, the angels and the devils had not seen the light of the day, the prophets and scriptures were not proclaimed, the paradise and hell were not conceived, the jinn and men were not shaped. Nature's brush was not dipped in colors, life was not skirted with spirit, chips of green and yellow had not piled up, life had not weaved the psyche's texture, the gardens of perceptions and notions had not bloomed. Pious were not fed upon the truth of milk, the pale of knowledge did not stretch beyond horizons, the skin in the bark of God's tree did not grow, the tongue did not leap up and blazed. The ego and the fuel of mind did not clutch the heart, the vowels of prowess did not weld the consonants, the birds had not learnt the art of prayers, the angels had not bowed before Adam and man had not fallen groveling at Lord's mercy. At that glorious and gracious moment there was nothing save the Magnificent Glitter of Lord's Countenance everywhere. There was light here and there, light left and right, light front and back, light up and down, light near and yonder, light vertically and horizontally, light diagonally and side wise, light in the north and the south, light in the east and the west and light upon light in all spheres and in all directions. Almighty God was self-sufficient, self-conscious, self-illuminating, self-existing, and self-adoring. His Essence was exalted, His Majesty was superb, His sovereignty was Absolute, His Uniqueness was perfect, His Supremacy was Infinite and His excellence was Eternal. There was God, without a prior or posterior, without a second or peer and without beginning and end, unborn and undying, devoid of affinities, formless and flawless and All-pervading. He was without and within, Omnipresent, Omniscient and Omnipotent, birth less, deathless and breathless, inconceivable and imperishable. He was alone, higher than the high, greater than the greatest, mightier than the mightiest, purer than the purest and most abiding in His greatness. For countless period He remained in the state of Unknowingness and Uniqueness as He deemed fit and when His Grandeur desired that He be known and adored, he pronounced, Be', and Lo! the Mighty Throne, the Slate of Destiny, the Mother Book, the Pen, the angels, the hell and the paradise, the heavens and the earth and the living and non-living and the perceptible and the imperceptible were there adoring and praising their Creator in obligation and thankfulness. The Lord in His Mercy and Beneficence finally created Adam and placed his spirit in him and ordered the angels to bow before him. Lo! all bowed down save the devil, the arrogant and the rejected.

THE BIRTH OF HOLY PROPHET

Several Prophets appeared upon the earth but in the lineage of Prophet Abraham and Prophet Ismail and in the house of Abdullah the son of Abdul Muttalib, there dawned such a majestic and the magnificent personality about whom several prophets had already foretold and whose pious and noble description was found practically in almost all the scriptures of the world. In the most noble family of Abdul Muttalib, gracious Amina the wife of Abdullah gave birth to that gifted personality in Makkah on April 22, 570 AD who was crowned as Muhammad (PBUH), means "often praised" or "worthy of praise" or "most praised".

It was this splendid and majestic child who was to be crowned as the 'Last Messenger of God,' the 'Mercy upon mankind' and the 'Ruler of one of the greatest empires of the world.' The Exalted Highness of Islam or the son of Abd Allah bin Abd al Muttalib bin 'Abd Munaf bin Quasayy bin Kilab's genealogy can be safely traced to the dignified tribe of Adnan and the house of Abraham in around fortieth decent. He had the noblest lineage on earth. His dreaded enemy Abu Sufyan attested to this fact in front of Heraclius, the ruler of Rome. This much awaited and foretold 'Being' was in much demand everywhere. The Jews were searching him in their tribes, the Christians were expecting him among their clans and the Sabians and Magians and others were sure of his dawn within their communities. The Magnificent personality was so important that it was to change the complex, character, shape and content of ideas, ideologies, belief systems and ways of living of the entire humanity for all times to come. The much loved and admired Grace and Glory was to appear upon the soil of Makkah during the renowned "Elephant Year" when the Lord had miraculously destroyed the arrogant might of Abraha Ashram by the flocks of birds who was bent upon destroying Kaaba. The monarchs, emperors, kings, rulers and the chiefs were anxiously looking at the fingers of clock when there was to emerge an exalted Guide who was to change the whole meaning, perception and conception of kingship and emperorship till eternity by his simplistic ways of living. The priests, rabies, monks, saints, temples, churches, monasteries and synagogues were looking at the Lord with keen interest when he was to send the 'Savior' of mankind who by his genius and intelligence was to raise the dignity of the Transcendent and the Immanent Lord to the new heights and lead humanity to the highest altitudes of pieties, glories and magnificence. The thinkers, philosophers and intellectuals were looking with extreme anxiety at the tickling time when a greatest genius had to dawn upon the earth who was to give a new philosophy of life to entire humanity which was drifting towards ruin and depravity. The reformers, idealists, humanists and guides were awfully waiting for such a noble soul who by his exemplary conduct and behaviour was to show such a path to humanity which was to provide them comforts and salvation both in this world and the hereafter.

PROCLAMATION OF HOLY PROPHET AS THE MAGNIFICENT RULER

The author felt that so much has been written in the past and so much would be written in the future by the pious, gifted and eminent thinkers, philosophers and world-fame writers about the Holy Prophet of Islam which was not written and which will not be written about any highly intellectual and gracious genius, most profound and greatest emperor, extremely beloved and compassionate leader and exceptionally gifted and immensely farsighted men on earth. The author would have never dared to enter where angels fear to tread had he not honestly and sincerely felt that advertently or inadvertently many prominent Muslim Jurists, eminent political thinkers, distinguished Muslim theologians and the best brains of mankind perhaps devoted lesser space in projecting the Holy Prophet of Islam as a Merciful Ruler compared to what they wrote about his multidimensional aspects. In the same way, they did not highlight the miracles of Holy Prophet as much as the miracles of Prophet Moses and Prophet Jesus were highlighted by their followers perhaps because Holy Prophet did not take the support of miracles to spread Islam. He propagated Islam by his conducts, practices and behaviour patterns. Likewise, they did not project him profusely and prominently as the Exalted Emperor of the Islamic state perhaps due to the fact that if they would have done so, the ordinary people would have thought that he was the torch bearer, friend and philosopher of the kings, emperors, monarchs and the highly placed persons and not the leader, sympathizer and savior of the commoners. Since they knew that most of the people from Muslim Umma would be poor, indigent and attached to the grass root level they projected him in poverty, impoverishment and strained conditions which enabled the impoverished, miserable and downtrodden Muslims to adopt him as their real leader, master and guide. The geniuses of Islam projected the poverty of the Holy Prophet as his privilege, hunger as his uniqueness, misery as his grace, struggle as his distinction and simplicity as his way of life and not as his weaknesses as a consequence of which whenever someone was hungry, miserable, poor and under odd conditions he did not consider his material drawbacks as the curses of God but the Sunna (practice) of Holy Prophet which lifted his morale and did not allow him to fall in his own eyes. It is also a fact that Holy Prophet never claimed himself as the Founder of Islamic State or the Emperor, King, Monarch, Ruler, Khalifa or Imam of the Islamic State and his learned and pious Companions too did not declare him so. The 'pious ruler' led a simple but purposeful life because God too did not want him to live the life of a hermit in the jungles or mountains or caves after abandoning the world for he was primarily sent as the Mercy to Mankind and he was to benefit humanity by living with them and solving their problems rather than merely remembering Lord in isolation. Similarly, Lord did not want him to enjoy the kingly life of monarchs in comforts and luxuries because he had come to the world to wipe the tears of orphans, salvage the widows, help the downtrodden and lead the mankind on the path of truth, justice and piety and not to indulge in comforts and luxuries. Moreover, through his simple and purposeful life he wanted to smash the prides, egos and the vanities of the kings, emperors, monarchs and others who in the name of the representatives of the Lord were falsely exploiting human beings as their stewards, saviors and protectors. He bestowed upon him the biggest kingdom of the world and destined him to live among commoners like an ordinary being with family and to share the troubles, sorrows and joys of life so that he could prove as a shining example for humanity as well as the guide to monarchs, kings, emperors, chiefs and rulers of the world.

All the above facts are true but the historical facts abundantly reveal that he was in fact a Grand Ruler of the Arabian Peninsula. It is a fact of history that he unilaterally established the Islamic State at Medina in 622 A.D. which after ten years covered whole of north Arabia and the people of the world recognized him as its leader, ruler, king, monarch and emperor. He fought battles and the wars, entered in alliances with other nations, met foreign envoys and dignitaries, wrote letters to kings, monarchs, rulers and emperors and controlled and managed the Islamic State as the Head of the State. That Head of the State certainly deserves some apt, appropriate and meaningful nomenclature in the light of the conventions, niceties and the etiquettes of the state craft. The author has merely endeavored to fill this gap.

Some Muslim Jurists and thinkers claim that the State which the Holy Prophet created was a democracy though different from Athenian one. Since the state belonged to God hence those who enforced and administered God's laws pertaining to the affairs of the Islamic state were to be considered as the representatives, Vicegerents or Khalifas of the Lord. On this analogy the Islamic Jurists declared the rulers of Islamic states as Caliphs rather than emperors. The author humbly submits that Holy Prophet can hardly be declared as Caliph as other Caliphs were known for neither he was elected nor designated as Caliph by the people of Arabia to run a state as other Caliphs of Islam were elected or found their places. Basically, he was the founder of the state. When the Prophet of Islam started his mission there were neither his followers nor the state. It was the Prophet of Islam who by the help of God unilaterally established the state or in other words God bestowed the kingship upon him in the same way as the kingships were given to Prophet David and Solomon and others by their Lord. Thus, he was the rightful ruler, king, monarch or emperor of the State and not its representative, Caliph or vicegerent as others were. It was due to his sweet will or on the advice of Lord that he did not transfer the state to his heirs as David transferred his kingdom to Solomon but handed it over to his people to be run and administered by them according to the Islamic principles. The fact is that all Kingdoms belong to Allah, He gives kingdoms whom he pleases and snatches sovereignties from whom he deems fit. He gave kingdoms to innumerable people including several prophets of Islam. The kingdoms were transferred between their heirs too and these prophets were known as kings, emperors, monarchs and rulers. The Holy Quran says, "Allah grants his kingdom to whom he pleases."[1] It further claims that "And David slew Jalut, and Allah gave him kingdom and wisdom and taught him what He pleased."[2] Not only this, the Holy Book certifies that the kingdom of David was inherited by Prophet Solomon. Quran certifies that "Solomon was David's heir."[3] Besides, Prophet Solomon too was known widely as the king because when Queen Sheba received the letter of Prophet Solomon asking her not to confront him but to submit before him, she told her courtiers that "Surely the kings, when they enter a town, ruin it and make the noblest of its people to be low and thus they (always) do. And surely I am going to send a present to them, and shall wait to see what (answer) do the messengers bring back."[4] The word 'king' that she used referred to Prophet Solomon. Thus, in the light of the above observations, the author could reverently address the Prophet of Islam as the Exalted Ruler of Islamic State. The author also has several proofs in support of the fact that Holy Prophet was known as the Emperor during his days of triumph. Michael H. Hart has called him as an "effective ruler of all southern Arabia."[5] Likewise, when 'Urwah met Quraish at the time of Treaty of Hudaibia he told them that "I have been to Chosroes in his kingdom, Caesar in his kingdom and the Negus in his kingdom, but never have I seen a king among a people like Muhammad among his companions."[6] Similarly, when Umar came to the house of Holy Prophet and saw half a Saa of barley in a container, a water skin that hung on the wall and Holy Prophet sitting on a hay mat which had left marks on his body, he wept bitterly. The Messenger of God asked: "Why are you weeping? He replied: 'Why shouldn't I weep. Khosrau and Caesar enjoy themselves in this world and the messenger of Allah only owns what I see.'"[7] This shows that heart to heart Umar considered the Prophet of Islam as the gracious Emperor of Arabia but was pained having seen him living under odd conditions. In the same way, when Abu Sufyan saw Holy Prophet marching towards Makkah with a mighty army he said to Al-Abbas, the uncle of the Prophet: 'O Abbas, your nephew has become a grand King!' It is also a historical fact that when Ad'ee at-Ta'ee, the son of Ha'tim at-Ta'ee saw the Prophet he was confused whether he was a Prophet or a King. Thomas Carlyle also considered him as an emperor. He said "They called him a prophet you say—No emperor with his tiaras was obeyed as this man in a cloak of his own clouting."[8] It would not be out of place to mention here that the Chinese Emperor Hong-Wu of the Ming Dynasty has also declared Holy Prophet as the King of all the Kings in his poem which reads as follows:

> Since the creation of the Universe,
> God had decreed to appoint,
> This great faith-preaching man,
> From the West he was born,
> He received the Holy Scripture,
> A Book of thirty parts,
> To guide all creation,
> King of all Kings,
> Leader of Holy Ones,
> With Support from Above,
> To Protect His Nation,
> With five daily prayers,
> Silently hoping for peace,
> His heart towards Allah,
> Empowering the poor,
> Saving them from calamity,
> Seeing through the darkness,
> Pulling souls and spirits,

Away from all wrongdoings,
A Mercy to the Worlds,
Traversing the ancient majestic path,
Vanquishing away all evil,
His Religion Pure and True,
Muhammad,
The Noble and Great one.

On the basis of these facts the author concluded that surely and certainly the Holy Prophet of Islam was considered by the people as the grand Ruler of Arabic peninsula though he behaved as the Last Messenger and a humble servant of God. The author begs Lord's mercy and forgiveness if he has inadvertently transgressed any limit.

THE TASK WAS EXTREMELY DIFFICULT

When the author became convinced that the Last Messenger was also the Grand Custodian of Islamic state, he started his work on the subject but it dawned upon him that the task was indeed highly difficult and perplexing. When he started collecting material from encyclopedias, libraries and history books about the greatest, mightiest and the most famous emperors and rulers of the world with a view to compare them with the Mighty Ruler of Islam, he came to the conclusion that it was a futile exercise because the standards which the Gracious Chief of Islam had set for the monarchs and the rulers of the world were so high that the worldly kings and emperors could not stand nearby him. Those emperors whom we call the greatest of all times looked mere pygmies before him by all standards they were not worthy of being called the emperors and monarchs. The author searched many sources but could not find any emperor in the annals of history like the Exalted Ruler of Islam who had willingly and smilingly set for himself such objectives to run the state which were most sublime and superhuman. He could not discover a single monarch like the Exalted Ruler of Islam who undertook the task of governing his people in a manner which was beyond human power. Similarly, he did not confront any sovereign power whose attitude towards life was so simple. One day when the Holy Prophet got up after sleeping on a mat, he had mat marks on his sides. His Companions told him to make bedding for him. Thereupon he replied that he had nothing to do with the world. He was like a way farer who rode a beast that stopped to take shade and rest under a tree, and then left it behind and continued on the journey. In the record books, the author did not find any king who accomplished his stupendous task within so little time and such least efforts as the Chief of Islam did. He never found any ruler in human chronicles who had no means save himself and no aid except his handful companions but turned out to be the unique, exemplary and unmatchable ruler of all times. The author could not find any ruler in the four corners of the world who despite being the Ruler of Arabian Peninsula decided not to wear any crown, not to sit on any throne, not to grace any kingly robe and not to enjoy the paraphernalia of the state. The author has yet to discover an exemplary ruler who did not take any help from public exchequer and when he died he did not leave any Dirham or Dinar or slave but a white mule, his weapons and a piece of land that too he gave in charity. One can imagine how difficult it was to write about such an exceptional Ruler, ideal Chief, peerless Head and the rarest ruler who had no parallel, no competitor, no similar and no identical.

Moved by the simplicity, honesty and sincerity of the Ruler of Islamic state, when the author undertook the noble task and entered in the sacred territory of writing something about him as the Exalted Guide of Islam with awe and reverence, new avenues were opened, mysteries intensified, complexities deepened and he was completely aghast. The more the vistas were unrevealed, the more he realized that he was too far from the threshold of reality. He was at the verge of abandoning the pious venture but the inner joy and the sense of wonder and charm which the exemplary conduct of the Savior of Islam generated in his heart prevailed upon his limitations and hesitations. The rare moments of ecstasy provided him the much needed support. He mustered enough courage though he was conscious of the fact that to write about one who was on the top in precedence was next to impossible. He knew that not only the canvas of the task was wide but its inner meanings were deep and the marvelous mysteries of the venture were insurmountable. The author admits that he has not succeeded in doing justice to the task but he is convinced that God willing, exceptional and the wonderful works on the subject by geniuses from among the exceptional, intelligent and enlightened people would soon see the light of the day.

HOLY PROPHET WAS A UNIQUE MAN OF HISTORY

It is most unfortunate that over 14 centuries since the advent of Islam, Holy Prophet, his life and his religion have been exhibited negatively due to doctrinal and political reasons. It is irony of fate that every aspect of the life and the message of the Holy Prophet have been made the subject of debate and discussion with critics pouring venom. The success of Muslim armed forces across West Asia, North Africa and even Europe after the demise of the Holy Prophet made the enemies of Islam see Muslims as despised, others with the Prophet of Islam being portrayed over centuries as the unholy man of the history. Those who have written favourably about him too have not shied away from depicting some of his strategic and noblest acts as unsavory. The currents of Islam phobia in many parts of the contemporary Western world, strengthened by the events of 9/11 and supported by extremist violence increased the number of critics of the Holy Prophet to many fold. However, the bright aspect of the situation is that there are innumerable faithful in the world who see him not only as the most ideal and perfect human being but also a unique man of all times as well as the Last Messenger of God. It is a fact that many intellectuals of world fame believe that Holy Prophet was destined to become not only the rarest of the rare but the highest of the high, greatest of the greats and the noblest among all the nobles that the created world had ever produced. Even those who do not believe him as the Messenger of God confess that by his exemplary conduct, beautiful thoughts, excellent deeds and marvelous behaviour he changed the entire course of human history. Those who are his extreme critics do not deny the fact that he was a unique personality, a very distinguished human being and a greatest genius the like of whom the mankind had never seen before. Those who have read his biography are convinced that by his firmness of aims, meagerness of means, humbleness of manners and astounding results he changed the map of the world till the Day of Reckoning. Even his adversaries agree that his strong faith, convincing words, marvelous deeds and exemplary conducts were more powerful than the weapons of steel and he was Cyrus and Pope in one but without the mighty army and the nobles of the emperor and the pomp and show of the pontiff. Humanity cannot cite any personality greater than the Ruler of Islam for he was not only the greatest leader of all times but a rare phenomenon on earth walking in flesh and blood and having the maximum impact through ages. He exercised such a tremendous and healthy influence upon human race which was never exercised by any leader, statesman, politician, reformer and rich and famous man on the globe. Besides, his impact as the saviour of human race was so formidable that it shall not be forgotten by posterity till the days and nights survive.

It is misery that the critics of Islam did not calmly and patiently ponder over his contribution. If they would have done so they too would have certainly bowed before his multidimensional personality. History is witness to the fact that no man in the annals of the recorded chronicles has been praised and respected so much since creation of the world as the Holy Prophet of Islam. Innumerable people live and die for him, numberless aspire to see the mere reflection of his last abode of peace, multitude remember him day and night and look towards him as their only Messiah in this world as well as the only saviour in the life after death. He is showered praise everyday by the Lord and His angels and every faithful utters "May Peace be upon him" when his name is mentioned. The more we ponder over him, the more we realize that we know very little about him. Thirteen hundred or more years have passed during which innumerable kings and kingdoms have perished, infinite palaces and castles have been ruined, several cities and habitations have been decayed but the influence and impact of the Ruler of Islam continue to remain unabated. The writer like Michael H. Hart has given him top ranking among the hundred most influential persons in history. Hart has not only pronounced him as "the most influential political leader of all time." But has also declared him as "the most influential single figure in human history."[9]

NOTES

1. *Ibid.*, (2: 247).
2. *Ibid.*, (2: 251).
3. *Ibid.*, (27: 16).
4. *Ibid.*, (27: 34-35).
5. Michael H. Hart. "The 100—A Ranking of the most influential persons in history" (Meeraa Publication, India, 1999), p. 34.
6. Abdul Hameed Siddiqui. "The Life of Muhammad (m.p.b.u.h) Islamic Book Services (P) Ltd., New Delhi, 2012), p. 229.
7. Abdurrahman al-Sheha. "Muhammad the Messenger of Allah" (Islamic Propagation Office, Rabwah, 2005), p. 48.
8. *Ibid.*, p. 70.
9. Michael H. Hart. op. cit., pp. 39-40.

2

The Early Days of the Ruler of Islam at Makkah

The Ruler of Islam was unique and incomparable in several ways. He had a noble origin but was not born with silver spoon in his mouth. He was neither like Buddha, the son of the ruling king in Kapilavastu nor Asoka, the grandson of Chandragupta Maurya nor Mahavira who was brought up in luxury nor Augustus Caesar, the grandnephew of Julius Caesar nor Charlemagne whose grandfather was Charles Martel nor Cyrus the great whose parents were vassals of the king of the Medes nor Constantine the great whose father was a high-ranking army officer, nor George Washington who was the son of a wealthy planter. He was born as an orphan. Shortly after his birth he was handed over to Thuwaybah, a slave girl who fed as she had fed Hamzah, his uncle. Later on he was entrusted to Haleemah Abi Dhuaib, a Bedouin wet nurse from Bani Sa'd bin Bake who accepted him reluctantly. As time elapsed she discovered in the child miraculous qualities and she developed special affinity towards the child and left no stone unturned in nursing him according to the best customs, practices and traditions of affluent Arabs. The child grew up in the free and healthy surroundings of the desert too far away from the evils of sedentary life and acquired robust health and learnt chaste speech and pure manners of the Bedouins. During the period when he lived within the quiet serenity of country-side, the habits of meditation, aloofness and reflection which were part and parcel of his body, mind and soul further developed and which persisted throughout his life.

THE TRAINING PERIOD OF HOLY PROPHET

Holy Ruler lived comfortably with Haleemah and never forgot her even after he was separated from her. She used to meet him often and he helped her on several occasions with a flock of sheep, a noble riding camel, riches and gifts. When his foster-sister was brought before him as one of the captives in his expedition to Taif, he spread his mantle for her too and asked her to sit upon it. He persuaded her to live with him but when she expressed her desire to go back home, he gave her gifts and permitted her to live with her own people.

At the age of five he was finally returned to his mother. Unfortunately, his mother too lived with him till he was six years old. She took him with her to Medina in 576 A.D. and she died while returning from Medina. His grandfather looked after him but he too died when he was eight years, two months and ten days old. For forty years, he was brought up and looked after compassionately and carefully by his uncle Abu Talib.

We learn from the early life of the Chief of Islam that he was a thoughtful boy, he took care of his family and played with boys. He also spent much of his time alone in pondering about the welfare of people around him and the mysteries of nature. He observed that most of the people struggled for power and money and once they got them they cared least for the poor and the weak. The Custodian of Islam had no particular job during the days of his youth. It is claimed that he worked as a shepherd for Bani Sa'd in Makkah. Like other young boys of his age he tendered the goats and sheep of Makkah and grazed them on the neighbouring valleys and hills as Prophet Moses and Prophet David did during their childhoods. The faith in One Supreme God was inherently ingrained in his each hair, every cell, each vein, every artery, each drop of blood, every tissue, each limb and every part of the body including, heart, mind, soul, insight, conscience and thinking process and behaviour pattern. While sitting on the lonely rocks, when he looked above, the pillar less dome of the sky, the endlessness of the space and the mysteries of nature compelled him to admire the beauty of the creator. When his eyes turn to the burning desert, the shifting sand dunes and the beautiful waves on the barren chest of the mighty desert reminded him the magnificent glory of the Lord. When the night darkened and he glanced at the twinkling stars, beautiful constellations gliding through the sky, he was immensely impressed by the grandeur of God. When the thunder broke the silence and the lightening brightened the darkness, he realized that there was an Al-pervading and magnificent Lord who was ruling the heavens and the earth. Wherever he looked he was delighted. He found tongue in every leaf, voice in every atom and a supreme commanding power everywhere. He reflected on the rising and declining sun and the moon, lengthening out of shadows, alternation of days and nights, varieties of languages and dialects and shapes and forms of men and women and came to firm conclusion that there was a Master Mind that was controlling everything. He searched the truth among the created phenomenon, found the presence of God in every event and entity and observed infinite love of God in the movements of insects, smell of the herbs, beauty of fruits, taste of vegetables, shades of trees and usefulness of plants, variety of animals and piety of human beings. The love for meditation, seclusion and reflection took him to great heights till he was guided by the Lord through the medium of revelation.

The Chief of Islam faced the realities of the phenomenal world at his earliest age. In the year 582 A.D., when he was at the age of twelve, he undertook a journey to Syria along with his uncle Abu Talib. It was during this journey that Bahira, a Christian monk perceived in him the symptoms of a Messenger whom the people were waiting for too long and he advised his uncle not to allow him to come in the contact of Jewish Rabies and return to Makkah as early as possible which he did. It was at the initiative of his uncle Abu Talib that at the age of 25 years he went to Syria in 594 A.D. as a merchant for Khadijah bint Khwailid who was a rich, famous and renowned business-woman. His honesty, truthfulness and trustworthiness impressed Khadijah immensely and she married him in 595 A.D.

HIS RAREST QUALITIES

If one looks at the life history of the Steward of Islam, one would be more than convinced that a child born as an orphan and brought up as orphan and that too in a family which did not have any lineage with kings and emperors could never dream of becoming one of the most powerful and influential Rulers of his time. Admittedly, he possessed in his self all those qualities in super abundance which make a man righteous, just, truthful, trustworthy as well as a gracious, majestic and compassionate king. Many people's attention did not go towards his exceptionally bright qualities of leadership and statesmanship such as farsightedness, resoluteness, courage and conviction which were in themselves more than enough to elevate him to that position. Many Christian monks knew about him more than their sons and a few of them had already recognized him. Likewise, Jewish rabies knew that he had arrived and was destined to leave his permanent impact upon mankind for all times to come. There is no doubt that the child born at Makkah was an exceptional child. It was unbelievable that without formally knowing reading, writing and arithmetic, he was extremely wise, thoroughly genius and immensely expert in all fields as he conducted all the functions of statehood with utmost competence, ease and dexterity. Similarly, without learning the social, cultural and moral traits and etiquettes within the four walls of his house or in nearby training centre, he taught the niceties of life, refined manners and the ways of living of the kings and commoners alike. He proved to be one of the most competent Rulers of his times without attending any class on the art of governance. Likewise, he showed his valour as the commander on the battle field without getting any military training. No business school taught him the good principles and practices to do business but he managed the business affairs of Khadijah for whom he acted as an agent most effectively, most honestly and most profitably. During his childhood also he seldom participated in riding, tent packing, arrow throwing, sword practicing and games and sports but when he fought the fierce battles his dreaded army generals bowed their heads before his expertise.

He never participated in debating competition, no guru taught him how to make friends and influence people but by his extraordinary oratory and immaculate communication skill he won the hearts of the people for all times to come. Since his childhood it appeared that he had a natural disposition to become the exalted emperor, dashing and brave commander, exemplary leader, able statesman, talented business magnate, compassionate ruler, reliable colleague, trusted friend, pious preacher and wonderful human being. His best and commendable social attributes, weighty mind and faultless insight were visible from his child days. He was bestowed with super intelligence, innovative ideas, noble thoughts and accurate choice of appropriate means leading to the achievement of the desired objectives. He was inclined to keep quiet and his long silence helped him to meditate and move in search of the truth. His pure nature, clarity of mind and spotless conscience helped him to deal with individuals, groups, societies and monarchs amicably on his own terms. He shunned idol worshipping, superstitious practices and evil and sinful acts. He never participated in drinking wine, lusty entertainments, games of chance and eating meat slaughtered on stone altars. He either participated in constructive activities or resorted to the solitude in search of eternal truth. He was renowned for his modest behaviour, virtuous and spotless character and graceful manners. He was sincere in his talk, honest in dealings and most obliging. He was most hospitable to guests, gentle-hearted in charity, mildest in temper and straightforward in commitment. He did not have much experience of the real world but guided the whole mankind on the path of truth, justice, piety and good conscience.

He kept himself away from violence, vulgar habits, indecency, voluptuousness and vices of those days that were rampant among his compatriots. He never indulged in pride, vanity, anger, revenge and foul play. He hated humiliating, belittling and insulting others. He disliked arrogance, injustice, discrimination and partiality in any field. He abhorred bloodshed, quarrelling, hatred and pomp and show. He always remained fair and honest in his dealings and impressed people with his purity of thoughts, simplicity in manners and decency in conducts. He was thoroughly trustworthy, extremely affectionate, intensely kind and utmost helpful and intimately sympathetic to colleagues needy, downtrodden and the wayfarers. He was perfectly faithful in matters of trusts and promises. His wise council, wonderful gesture, marvelous posture and beautiful body language impressed every one beyond limits. By his honesty, sincerity, piety and unobtrusive youth he earned the title of the "Truthful" and "Trustworthy" or "Sadiq" and "Ameen".

He did not receive his higher education from universities as Isaac Newton, Martin Luther and Galileo received and did not attend any university to get his Ph.D. degree as Karl Marx, Albert Einstein and Louis Pasteur did. Besides, he did not study under any teacher as St. Paul studied under Rabbi Gamaliel, Aristotle under Plato and Lenin from Marx. The Islamic traditions narrate that he did not receive his formal education from any school, madersa, college, university, institute or person. Since he had not attended any teaching, coaching or training classes, many people ignorantly considered him unlettered though the world has seen that he "rehearsed the verses of Holy Quran among people, taught scripture and wisdom and purified them."[1] Likewise, he did not get any formal or informal military training as George Washington got by serving in the army and taking active part in the French and Indian War, Napoleon Bonaparte got his training in military academies of France, Adolf Hitler served in German army and was wounded and received medals for bravery and Sui wen Ti received his first military appointment when he was only fourteen years old.

He never raised any army to subdue people as Genghis Khan had raised a formidable military machine to conquer people, Hitler led Germany on the path of conquests that was to generate World War II and Cyrus the great built a big military might for foreign conquests. He never invaded any country, neighbour, land or region with a view to obtain territory as William, the conqueror did to obtain the throne of England, Asoka attacked Kalinga to have control over east coast of India, Charlemagne conquered Saxony and founded the Holy Roman Empire and Alexander, the great wanted to invade Arabia, India, Rome, Carthage, and western Mediterranean to become the conqueror of the world. Interestingly, nobody had any grievance against him due to any misadventure on his part or some kind of injury inflicted by him in the past or some sort of revenge nurtured against him or any immediate threat to their territories from his side for by all world standards he was an insignificant person, a father-less son facing odd conditions in life. It is highly puzzling that from a non-entity he became all in all and despite not fighting any aggressive war he became the conqueror of whole of southern Arabia. It appears that his dreaded enemies made him the Emperor of their lands because had they not attacked him and got defeated in all wars they fought, Holy Prophet would have never succeeded in establishing one of the biggest empires during the shortest period of his life.

HE WAS BORN AMONG FIERCE AND FIERY PEOPLE

Holy Prophet was neither born in any important city like Athens, the abode of democracy nor in Rome the cradle of civilization nor in Jerusalem the convergence of various cultures. Similarly, like many eminent personalities such as Mani, Peter the great and Machiavelli he was neither born in any socially, culturally and economically advanced areas like Mesopotamia, Moscow and Florence nor among any highly civilized, advanced and enlightened people like Persians, Czars and Italians but in a far flung backward, arid, waterless, unfriendly, barren and hilly area away from the centers of trade, culture, learning and civilization and surrounded by blazing desert and blasting sun. He was born among people who were fiery in temper, ardent in love of their idols, bitter in hate, fierce in wars and unmatched in ignorance and superstition and blood-thirsty in taking revenge. They loved flashing swords, deadly lances and piercing arrows and moved with fastest speeds on horses and camels. When he opened his eyes he found himself surrounded by people who were merged in superstition, ignorance and false beliefs. The society was divided into slaves and the masters, haves and have-nots and rulers and the subjects. They boasted of their tribes and clans, considered themselves as eloquent and others as deaf and dumb. They exploited the slaves, women and children and indulged in all types of atrocities, sins and wickedness. Drinking had become their second habit. They found solace in wine and as a result of licentious drinking fornication was very rampant. Prostitution and indecency were widespread and adultery and obscenity prevailed among all segments of the society. Girls imported from Syria and Iraq entertained the rich and famous people and decency and modesty had been swept away from the society. Polygamy, polyandry and debauchery had overshadowed all other human relations. Arabs had little regard for the sanctity of matrimonial alliances. Men were overlords and the women lived under bondages. Men folk took pride in their adulterous activities. There was no check on the number of wives and men could marry as much as they could afford and leave them when they deemed fit. The inter-tribal relations were very fragile and the clans and the tribes fought bloody wars against one another on minor matters such as on getting lead in a horse race or winning a game of chance. Women were considered as chattels and marketable properties and they were sold to the highest bidders. Female infanticide was followed as a normal practice since young girls were considered as the symbols of disgrace and they were buried alive due to poverty and ignominy of marrying them to other males. The Arabs were mostly pagans and they believed in many gods except a few Jews and Christians who were on their religion.

ATROCITIES ON HOLY PROPHET AND HIS FAMILY MEMBERS

Despite opening his eyes in such a surrounding, he glittered on the horizon of whole of Arabia as a blazing sun of grace and glory. Before declaring himself as the Messenger of God, Holy Prophet remained among Arabs of Makkah for forty years as an ordinary man. He lived among his people with all aspects of his life wide open. All called him, truthful, merciful, just, compassionate, bringer of good tidings and excellent in conduct. They considered him as hard honest, extremely pious and most trust worthy. Even while addressing them from Mount As Safa when he said "If I were to tell you that there were some horsemen in the valley planning to attack you, will you believe me?" They replied "Yes, we have never observed you lying." However, when he declared that their gods were false and the only God worthy of worshipping was Allah with no associate, they became hostile and adopted a hostile attitude towards him, his clan, his followers and his sympathizers.

The Quraish of Makkah called a meeting of twenty-five prominent Arabs as important as Abu Jahal and decided to teach lessons to Holy Prophet and his followers. They called him poet, magician, madman and priest and leveled different charges against him. His own uncle Abu Lahab and his wife Umm Jameel bint Harb left no stone unturned in harming and harassing him. Abu Lahab dealt him a severe blow below his belt by forcing his two sons to divorce their wives called Ruqaiya and Kulthum who were the beloved daughters of the Holy Prophet. Abu Lahab's wife too did not lag behind. She made it a practice to throw thorns tied with twisted palm leaf fibers on the path of the Prophet. She not only hatched defamatory plots, initiated a campaign of hatred, indulged in scandal mongering, backbiting and spite but also did not hesitate to throw stones at him. At the dirty initiative of Abu Lahab, Uqbah bin Abi Mu'ait dared to throw the filthy fetus of a she camel on the back of the Prophet while he was praying at Holy Kabah.[2] Ubai bin Khalaf went to the extent of blowing the powder of old decomposed bones at the face of Prophet to quench his hunger for revenge. He asked 'Uqbah bin Al-Mu'ait to spit on the glorious and the gracious face of the Holy Prophet which shamefully he did. Utaibah bin Abi Lahab once came to the Holy Prophet and arrogantly shouted at him, laid violent hand upon him, tore his shirt and tried to spit on his face. It is also stated that when the Prophet of Islam was prostrating in prayers Uqbah bin Abi Mu'ait rode on his neck put his garment around his neck and throttled him violently but Abu Bakr intervened and saved him. Abu Jahal once took a big rock in his hand and was to drop on the head of the Holy Prophet while he was praying but the rock fell from his hands due to unknown fear. Abu Jahal was a constant enemy. He used to plan his conspiracies by inciting people and throwing dust on the face and the back and making all the efforts to banish the Prophet of Islam from the sanctuary of Makkah. In order to remove him from the scene, they went to Abu Talib the uncle of the Prophet and persuaded him to exchange his nephew for a young and a smart boy. When his uncle declined to do so, they finally decided to remove him from the scene for ever. However, prior to killing him they lured him by offering all types of temptations. When they failed, they held a meeting and formed a confederation hostile to Bani Hashim and Bani Al-Muttalib. In 616 A.D., they decided to boycott them and not to have any business, family, marriage and other social relations with them including visits and verbal contacts. Abu Talib intelligently shifted towards a valley on the eastern outskirts of Makkah. Banu Hashim and Banu Al-Muttalib also followed him. Nearly for three years they remained confined to a narrow pass unaided. The supply of food was stopped and people from outside were debarred from approaching them.

Consequently, they had to eat leaves of trees and the skins of the animals. Sometimes the cries of the children due to hunger were heart-breaking but despite all these obstacles the Prophet of Islam did not deviate from his mission. Seeing them in a pitiable condition resentment started growing among Meccans who were the relatives of the Banu Hashim and Banu Al-Muttalib and finally the boycott was lifted. The Quraish made a last try by reaching to Abu Talib when he was sick on bed and offered before him that they would not interfere with Muhammad (PBUH) and he should not interfere with theirs but it was not accepted by the Prophet of Islam. It was indeed the unshakable faith in Allah that the Holy Prophet of Islam and his followers bore all types of inhuman persecutions but never deviated from their path. The Quraish persecuted all sections of society including those who were from higher strata and who had embraced Islam. Many of them were wrapped in the raw skins of camels and thrown away on high ways and a few of them were put in armours and cast on burning sand in the hot noon. The persecutions upon Muslims started from the fourth year of Prophet hood and by the middle of the fifth year it became difficult to face them. Seeing the humble and weak Muslims in extreme trouble Holy Prophet advised some of them to go to Abyssinia which was ruled by a pious Christian King named Ashamah Negus. Under cover of darkness sixteen of them slipped away, to be followed latter by another eighty-three men and women. The pagans could not tolerate that Muslims lived in peace anywhere. They sent powerful envoys to Abyssinia for their extradition but could not succeed due to the merciful attitude of the King. For thirteen long years Holy Prophet tolerated the persecution for no other reason but inviting people towards the right path. History is witness to the fact that Buddha and Mahavira and many saints in China and Europe were hailed for preaching their belief systems but the tortures and agonies which the Prophet of Islam faced were unprecedented in the history of the prophets of the world.

It is irony of fate that the Holy Prophet of Islam did not harm any section of the society by his words, deeds and conducts yet he was subjected to unprecedented tortures. What he said and preached was neither against any king nor emperor nor state nor kingdom nor society nor person. The gist of his message was: "worship one true God, the real Master of this universe instead of worshipping innumerable, false, man-made gods. Behave kindly with people and consider the life, honour and property of every person worthy of respect. Adopt the best manners in dealing with relatives, respect the elders and treat the minors in an affectionate manner. Render help to the weak and the needy, abhor bad habits like lying, deceit, backbiting and tale-bearing and avoid filthy and soiled things."[3] He said the same things which were told by other prophets, saints, warners and reformers. He told them to control their whims, greed and desires and not to envy, provoke and look down at each other. He forbade them from committing suicides, killing girls within wombs, degrading females and annoying their fellow beings. He stopped them from taking the lives of the innocent people, killing people for revenge and harming animals. He told them to live like civilized human beings and not to gamble and not to participate in anti-social activities. He advised them not to exploit, harm and betray others but be kind and merciful to human beings. He stopped people from giving and taking of interest and asked them to help those who are in financial distress. He reminded the people to give the labourers their wages before their sweats were dried. He checked people from giving and taking of bribes, following corrupt practices or doing those things of which they would have felt ashamed if they became known. He emphasized on covering up of the failings of their friends and not to reveal their weaknesses. He also told them not to be cruel to children, aged, handicapped and womenfolk. He encouraged them to gladden the heart of the afflicted, feed the hungry, remove the wrongs of the injured and provide comfort to the sorrowful. He impressed upon them to show proper respects to men in authority and shower compassion upon those who were under them. He told them not to take the money which rightfully belongs to the poor and orphans and not to usurp the trust of others. He asked them to help the widows, divorcees, sick, old and handicapped. He convinced the people that there was life after death and everyone would be answerable to what he did in this world and would be dealt with accordingly. He guided people on the path of sanity but never compelled anybody to accept his religion. It appears that what he said was not something entirely new. The humanity had heard it before. However, the result of his preaching was that he was so much tortured and troubled as none was done before. For thirty days and nights he and Bilal had nothing to eat save what could be hidden under the curve of Bilal's shoulders. The Quraish used to throw blood soaked clothes from ladies menses, rotten skins and fetus of animals on his gate.

The Prophet of Islam started preaching Islam in 613 A.D. Initially, during the first three years of his mission he did not succeed in gathering a mighty army of his followers for the earliest converts were his wife Khadijah, his first cousin Ali, his servant Zeyd and his old friend Abu Bakr. The converts of the first four years were mostly the poor and the humble people who were weak enough to defend themselves. The Quraish of Arabia got frightened by his simple but piercing message and left no stone unturned in harming his members of family, colleagues and followers. When Abu Bakr accepted Islam notorious Quraish surrounded him and started beating him with their shoes. Blood oozed from his nose and face and he fell on the ground. It was because of the intervention of kinsmen that Abu Bakr was saved from their clutches. They subjected the Chief of Islam to every type of cruelty and insult. Thorns were strewn in his path, stones were thrown at his house, and the dirt and rubbish was pelted upon his face and body. He was laughed and ridiculed. They even planned to liquidate him in 622 A.D. The world history cannot show a single example of the mercy and the magnanimity which the Ruler of Islam showed when he conquered Makkah. He not only forgave his dreaded enemies who caused him immense harm but declared general amnesty to all Meccans including those who took shelter in the house of Abu Sufyan who was his dreaded enemy. The author searched for such an Emperor in the annals of history but came to the conclusion that the world has rightly said that the Ruler of Islam was the greatest among the greats and the superb and finest among the created world.

When the Prophet of Islam realized that the crooked Meccans were not going to hear him, he shifted his attention from Makkah to Ta'if. In the year June 619 A.D., he set out at Ta'if, a place about 60 Kilometers from Makkah along with his freed slave Zayd bin Haritha and approached one of the noblest families of 'Umayr but of no avail. He stayed there for ten days and tried his best to bring people to sanity and piety but failed miserably. With the intention to compel the Prophet of Islam to leave Ta'if at every cost, the people of Ta'if resorted to dirty tricks. They hooted him, shouted at him, abused and stoned him and compelled him to leave the streets of the city. Not only this, they followed him by relentless rabbles, blood flowing down his legs and filling his shoes. They injured him on the head, hands, neck, shoulders and on every part of the limbs. Zayd tried to shield him by wounding his head but with no gain.[4] The mob did not desist but chased them in scorching heat two to three miles across the sandy plains to the foot of nearby hills. Wearied and exhausted, he finally took shelter near the vineyard of Utbah and Shaybah, the sons of Rabi'ah a wealthy citizen of Makkah. The Ta'if time had been the worst period in his life time but he did not curse people and did not take revenge from people when in less than ten years he reached the spot as the mighty Commander and the head of the conquering army to destroy the idols of Ta'if. Finally, he decided to meet the individuals and the tribes nearby Makkah and conveyed to them his message. The result was encouraging. Many prominent individuals and tribes came within the fold of Islam. It encouraged him to expand his mission. People from far and wide also started meeting him among them were some people who were from Medina. They were so impressed that they embraced Islam and spread it at Medina.

MIGRATION OF HOLY PROPHET TO MEDINA

Despite the fact that Prophet's experience of Ta'if was horrible he did not lose hope. He adopted a multi-pronged strategy to spread his message among different segments of the society with a view to bring them within the fold of Islam. He approached all those tribes that were living near Makkah and which used to come to Kabah at the time of pilgrimage and emphasized upon them the need of abandoning the worship of the idols. He also addressed people at Ukaz, Makkah and Mina and other places and appealed people to give up idolatry and accept the sovereignty of the True Lord. It was during this period that he met six or seven people from Medina from a tribe of Kharraj. Since they had been hearing from the Jews in Medina that a Prophet was to come among them who would empower them, they believed in the Messenger ship of the Prophet and embraced Islam. On their return, they wholeheartedly preached Islam among their neighbours. On the following year at the time of the pilgrimage there came twelve people, ten from Khazrhaj and the two of the tribe of Aws and they took the pledge that they would worship none but Allah and follow Muhammad as his Last Messenger. Since this oath was taken at a little terraced mound, it is known as the First Pledge of 'Aqabah. Holy Prophet sent Mus'ab bin, 'Umayr bin. Hashim along with them so that he might teach them the principles and the practices of Islam. The result of Mus'ab's efforts was that Islam spread from house to house, family to family and individuals to individuals and the Jews remained dumb founded. Next year during pilgrimage time eighty-eight people from Medina took the oath at the same place and embraced Islam in its entirety which is known as the Second Pledge of 'Aqabah. After this Pledge since a considerable number of people had come within the fold of Islam, Holy Prophet encouraged people to migrate to Medina from Makkah. Within two months almost all the Muslims except Holy Prophet, Abu Bakr, Ali and those who were slaves or unable to move left Makkah for Medina. Even those who had gone to Abyssinia came to Medina. The large-scale migration of Muslims from Makkah to Medina perturbed the Quraish. They tried their best to stop as many people as possible and those who were bent upon going had to pay a heavy price. Finally, the Holy Prophet also migrated along with Abu Bakr on the command of God leaving 'Ali behind to return to their rightful owners the cash, ornaments and properties which the people had entrusted to Holy Prophet.

PERSECUTIONS OF THE FOLLOWERS OF ISLAM

Having known about the fact that Holy Prophet and his companions had succeeded in escaping to Medina they started persecuting those poor and helpless Muslims who were left behind. They invented torturous methods to harm and immobilize the faithful. Some were mercilessly bitten with iron rods till the blood oozed from their bodies, a few were dragged with chords around their necks through the main streets of the city to terrorize others from embracing Islam, many were compelled to lie down on the burning sand of Arabia with heavy load on their chests, a select band of people were tossed up on embers and there was no dearth of people who were wrapped in the raw skins of the camels and thrown on the road-sides. Eminent Muslims like Uthman bin Affan were not immune from atrocities. His uncle initially tied the hands of Uthman with ropes and did not allow him to go out and mingle with Muslims. When he continued to go he used to wrap Uthman in a mat of palm leaves and set fire under him which withered his skin.[5] In the same way, the uncle of Zubair bin Awwam wrapped the mat around his body and put it on fire to generate smoke in order to persuade him to abandon Islam. Talha bin Ubaidullah was subjected to unprecedented tortures. His hands used to be tied to his neck and he was dragged on the ground mercilessly. Bilal ibn Rabah, the slave of Omaiyah bin Khalaf was not only deprived of food and water for a considerable period of time but was also thrown down on the sand under the burning sun and kept there with a heavy stone on his chest.[6] The only words he uttered were "Ahad", "Ahad" and "Ahad" that is Allah, the One, the One and the One. He was also dragged by putting a chord around his neck through the hilly portion of Makkah. Amir, a freed slave of Bani Makhzoum and his father too were not spared. They were constantly beaten merciless by compelling them to lie on the burning sand. Yasar, the father of Ammar on embracing Islam could not face the tortures and died due to perpetual persecutions. Abdulla bin Huzafa never deviated from Islam despite so many threatening methods adopted on him. Abu Jahal became the cause of the death of Ammar's mother. The fate of Abu Fakeeh Aflah, a freed slave of Bani Abd As-Dar was miserable. He too was very often dragged throughout the streets of Makkah by tying his feet to a rope. The Meccans showed no mercy for Khabbab bin Al Aratt. To prevent him from accepting Islam, they used to pull his hair, roast his neck and made him lie on burning coal with a big stone on his chest. When Abu Zar Gaffari declared that he had accepted Islam, he was severely beaten to the extent that he was at the verge of death but was saved by onlookers. Musab bin Ameer had to face the tortures of enemy prison because of embracing Islam. When Abu Salamah decided of migrating, his in laws detained his wife, snatched his son and dislocated his hand. Uhaib, a wealthy businessman was allowed to leave Makkah only when he surrendered all his wealth, properties and possessions. Likewise, Abu Jahal tied the hands of Ayyash and did not allow him to leave Makkah for Madinah. Holy Prophet was highly worried because not only his followers were being targeted and persecuted at Makkah but people like Abu Lahab despite being his relative were insulting and humiliating his uncle Abu Talib and the Meccans had made it a point to harm as much as possible to Bani Hashim and Bani Al Muttalib. Al-Aswad son of Muttalib and his friends used to mock at the followers of Islam by saying: "The future kings of the world are here! They are going to conquer Kisra and

Caesar." Then they would burst into laughter and clap and whistle. These persecutions and taunts prevented others from embracing Islam. It is worth noting that Muslims tolerated all types of persecutions but remained steadfast and never reacted even in self-defence which in the long run brought about revolution in the minds, bodies and souls of Meccans and when they got the opportunity they joined Islam in multitude.

The above facts about the life of the Holy Ruler amply manifest that he was indeed the pioneer and the champion of non violence. History cannot show a single example prior to him of any Emperor, Ruler, Leader, Statesman or Human being who along with his members of family as well as friends and well wishers faced unprecedented persecutions at the hands of his enemies for the cause of uplifting mankind from the morass of ignorance but did not raise his hands against his adversaries. He continued his noble objectives under all strains facing all types of agonies and finally succeeded in his sacred task. The later centuries have seen a few glaring personalities who also championed the cause of non violence but none succeeded in reaching to the height of Holy Prophet. It appears that many of them took guidance from the exemplary conduct of the dignified Prophet and for many he shall prove as a guide, leader and champion of non violence.

NOTES

1. Holy Quran (2: 129).
2. Safiur Rahman al-Mubarakpuri, Ar-Raheeq Al-Akhtum. "The Sealed Nector" Biography of Noble Prophet. (Maktaba Dar-us-Salam Publishers and Distributors, Saud Arabia, 1995), p. 94.
3. Periodic golden history of Islamic conquest Atlas of the Islamic conquest from the Caliphate of Abu Bakr to the height of Ottomon Caliphate from Central Asia to Morocco and Central Europe. Compiled by Ahmed Adil Kamal. Translations and Editions Samin stretch/Mohsin Faraini Maktab Darrussalam 2010 King Fahad National Library Cataloging—Publication data—Riyadh Page 30.
4. Safiur Rahman, *op. cit.*, p. 136
5. *Ibid.*, p. 96.
6. *Ibid.*

3

The Founder of Islamic State at Medina

The Flight from Makkah to Medina called "Hegira" is known as the turning point in the lives of the faithful as well as a beginning of Muslim era. The Prophet's journey from Makkah to Medina was the first real step in the world-wide spread of Islam. Holy Prophet arrived at Medina on Friday, September 27th, 622 A.D. The first thing that he did after reaching Medina was to establish the public worship of one true God as well as to lay down a Constitution for a Islamic State. He gave new social order with mosque as its base. It was here that the First Constitution and the First Charter of Human Rights were worked out and written down. With freedom of worship and conscience and justice and equality guaranteed to rich and poor, Muslims and non-Muslims and to humble and highly placed, Islam's message of peace, prosperity, piety and tranquility reached far and wide.

ESTABLISHMENT OF A NEW SOCIETY

The people of Medina recognized him as their Emperor, King, Monarch, Head, Leader, Chief and everything since they surrendered before him gladly, willingly and unconditionally. He organized the affairs of Medina as a statesman and the Islamic state came into existence on 622 A.D. under the leadership of Prophet Muhammad (PBUH). At first a very small one but in ten years it grew into the Empire of Arabia. According to Hart "When Muhammad died, in 632 A.D., he was the effective ruler of all of southern Arabia."[1] The Guide of Muslims was basically interested to bring people from the dark age to a new and a bright era. After migrating to Medina he gave prime importance to the establishment of a new society in a safe place.

He had to face several difficulties because there were various segments of favorable people as well as unfavorable beings with whom he had to deal with.

Essentially, he was surrounded by two types of Muslims at Medina, the Helpers and the Emigrants. Some of the Helpers were very rich, well settled and with ease with their lives but there were old enmities between them. As against this, the Emigrants from Makkah were mostly jobless and penniless. They were a burden upon the society and their number was increasing day by day due to giving the green signal to Meccan Muslims by the Holy Prophet to migrate to Medina. Likewise, there were two categories from among the non-believers. They included the polytheists of Medina and the surrounding tribes of Arabia as well as the Jews who had come to Medina after their persecution in Syria by the Byzantines and the Assyrians. Some of the polytheists were inclined to Islam but there were others who nursed deep hatred against Islam due to the disbelief deeply rooted in their hearts. The Jews had adopted the Arabian dress code and had captured the trade and commerce of Medina. They dared not to show their resentment and anger against Muslims openly but did not like Muslims from the core of their hearts. They were basically treacherous people and had their eyes on the wealth of Medina. Besides, these Jews and polytheists had their cordial relations with Quraish of Makkah and provided them all types of information about the Muslims and provoked them to attack them at their new abode.

The first thing that the Ruler of Islamic state did after his arrival in Medina in 622 A.D. was the construction of a Mosque at the very site where his camel knelt down after purchasing land belonging to two orphans. The dignified Prophet himself participated in the construction of the Mosque by carrying bricks and stones. The Mosque was not only the religious place but it was a Islamic Darbar and an Islamic

Centre where foreign envoys and dignitaries met and where Muslims were taught the doctrines of the new religion. He then tried to cement the ties of brotherhood among the Muslims of Medina, the Helpers or Ansars and the Al-Muhajrin or the Emigrants by establishing between them the code of brotherhood. The Emigrants were feeling lonely and helpless since they had left behind all they possessed at Makkah. The world has seen that the impact of the speech of the Holy Prophet upon a gathering of about ninety people was so immense that all of them became like real brothers sharing all that was with them including wealth, possessions, properties, women and resources. The brotherhood that he created between the Emigrants and the Helpers was so unique that the world had never seen before. For instance, Sa'd bin Sabi', a helper who was the co-brother of 'Abd al-Rahman bin 'Awf, the Emigrant told him that he was the richest man among the Helpers. He was glad to share his property half and half with him. He had two wives. He was ready to divorce one, and after the expiry of 'iddah' he might marry her. Abd al-Rahman was not willing to share anything neither his property, nor home nor wife. He blessed him and asked him to direct him to the market so that he might earn his fortunes with his own hands."[2] Similarly, several Helpers approached the Ruler of Islam with a request that their orchards too might be distributed among themselves and the Emigrants but he did not permit them to do so. The Helpers were extremely generous to their brother Emigrants and they expressed their help to them under all conditions. So cordial were the relations between the two strangers that they superseded the ties of blood hood and kinships. The believers under the guidance of their leader developed in them such traits of character which removed from amongst them enmities of centuries and made them kith and kin. The world knows that the Arabs were a warring, uncompromising and bloodthirsty people. They used to fight on minor matters and their enmities lasted over several generations. Through his spectacular and marvelous reform the Ruler of Islam changed their mindsets and bound them in the brotherhood of man which was based on justice, piety, love and humane and noble principles. He created a society which was neither ceremonial in nature, nor authoritative in content, nor cultist in shape nor priestly in spirit. It was spiritual relationship to create a just, equitable and pious society based on universal brotherhood of all people of the world. In his newly created society all people irrespective of their physical, geographical, social, economic and cultural backgrounds were equal in all respects. All were created by the same Lord and all had originated from Adam and Eve. Only those were great who were morally and spiritually good and who were righteous and pious and possessed excellent conducts. He abolished slavery, provided equitable rights to women, raised the status of parents, generated compassion for younger ones, made people aware about the rights of neighbours, companions, way-farers and poor and the needy. He asked them to behave nicely with slaves and those who were under them. He asked people not to indulge in criminal and sinful acts and those acts which were detrimental to the society. He laid down laws for those things which were permissible and those that were not permitted. He asked people to do good things and avoid bad things and invite people to do good and to avoid what was bad. He gave them dress code, etiquettes for civilized life, rules for decency and decorum and a complete way of life to achieve betterment in this world and hereafter. Such instances of mutual love and affection between believers are rarely found among the nations of the world and it was this cementing worldly and religious force between the Muslims that made them different in the eyes of others. No emperor in the world succeeded in giving a comprehensive social, economic, legal, cultural, political, moral, aesthetical and spiritual code to its subject as the Champion of Islam did.

THE FIRST FRIENDSHIP CHARTER OF ISLAMIC ALLIANCE

Having done so he turned towards the non-Muslim tribes and tried to establish friendly relations between them. He placed before the believers and the non-believers of Medina the First Charter of Islamic Alliance with a view to establish friendly relations with them. He did full justice to all signatories and took into consideration the interests of all parties but tried to ensure that pre-Islamic traditions, inter-tribal feuds and false belief systems might not sneak in or violate the new system which he was going to place before the humanity. The Treaty of friendship was so just, transparent and unique in nature the like of which the Arabs had not seen before. The main features of the treaty were as follows:

> In the name of Allah, the Most Beneficent, the Most Merciful.

This is a document from Muhammad, the Messenger of Allah, concerning Emigrants and Helpers in which he made a friendly agreement and properly stated the reciprocal obligations as follows:

> They form one group to the exclusion of other people. The Emigrants of Quraish unite together and shall pay blood money among themselves, and shall ransom honorably their prisoners. The Banu Awf unite together, as they were at first, and every section among them pays a ransom for acquitting its relative prisoners. (This clause is repeated with the same substance concerning Banu S'ida, Banu al-Harith, Banu Jusham, Banu al-Najjar, Banu 'Amr Banu 'Awf, Banu al-Nabit and Banu Aws) Believers shall not leave anyone destitute among them by not paying his redemption money or blood money in kind.

Whoever is rebellious or whoever seeks to spread enmity and sedition, the hand of every God-fearing Muslim shall be against him, even if he be his son. "A believer shall not kill another believer, nor shall support a disbeliever against a believer. The protection of Allah is one (and is equally) extended to the humblest of the believers. The believers are supported by each other. Whosoever of the Jews follows us shall have aid and succor; they shall not be injured, nor any enemy be aided against them. The peace of the believers is indivisible. No separate peace shall be made when believers are fighting in the way of Allah. Conditions must be fair and equitable to all. It shall not be lawful for a believer, who holds by what is in this document and believes in Allah and the Day of Judgment, to help a criminal nor give him refuge. Those who give him refuge and render him help shall have the curse and anger of Allah on the Day of Resurrection. His indemnity is not accepted.

Whenever you differ about a matter, it must be referred to Allah and to Muhammad."[3]

The above treaty in fact was a tripartite treaty between the Emigrants of Makkah, the Helpers of Medina and the Jews of the surrounding areas. A careful look at the contents of the document reveals that it was a comprehensive piece of understanding between various segments of the society living in Arabia with a purpose to combine them into a strong coalition different from the rest. It was not a mere reconciliation between various tribes but a secular constitution to infuse several people of various castes, creeds and nationalities professing different religions, speaking different dialects and having different perceptions into a strong nation based on values and sound principles. In a sense it was a constitution of a Islamic state in its embryonic stage consisting of different tribes possessing narrow tribal loyalties with a view to bring them within a solid superstructure of a state based on new religion. This treaty of alliance recognized the gracious Prophet not only as the sole arbitrator in the wake of any dispute but also accepted him as the controller of Medina and the architect of peace in the whole region. The treaty dividing the different segments of the society into Jews and Muslims highlighted the spirit of understanding between the Muslims and the non-Muslims based on piety, non-violence and peaceful co-existence. The treaty of alliance was a landmark contribution in the history of mankind because fourteen hundred years ago it guaranteed freedom of thought and worship to those people who were the victims of oppression, despotism and anarchy. It provided safety and security to life, property, possessions and honours and declared all crimes against humanity as illegal, inhuman and unwarranted. The genius of the Ruler of Islam lies in the fact that by his mere foresight, wisdom and love for mankind he gave the entire humanity a secular, just and humane constitution for good governance, harmonious co-existence and peace and progress especially in those days when nobody could dream of it.

THE COOPERATION AND NON-AGGRESSION PACT WITH JEWS OF MEDINA

After having satisfied that the foundations of the Islamic society were laid on firm ideological, administrative, political and cultural footings of Islam and a broad framework had been laid for peace between Muslims, Jews and warring tribes, the Holy Prophet turned to the non-Muslims of Medina especially the Jews who did harbor evil intentions and nursed bitter grudges but showed neither animosity nor resistance nor hostility openly. He tried his best to establish permanent, regular and clear-cut relations with the non-Muslims with a view to provide peace, prosperity and security to all people. Since geographically the Jews were living closest to Muslims he decided to ratify a treaty with the provisions that ensured full freedom in faith, belief system, wealth, worship and possessions.

The salient features of the "Cooperation and non-Aggression Pact with the Jews were as flows:

1. The Jews of Bani Awf are one community with the believers. The Jews will profess their religion and the Muslim theirs.
2. The Jews shall be responsible for their expenditure, and the Muslims for theirs.
3. No one shall go forth to war except with the permission of Muhammad; but this shall not hinder any one from seeking lawful revenge.
4. If attacked by a third party, each shall come to the assistance of the other.
5. Each party shall hold counsel with the other.
6. Mutual relation shall be founded on righteousness, sin is totally excluded.
7. Neither shall commit sins to the prejudice of the other.
8. The wronged party shall be aided.
9. The Jews shall contribute to the cost of war so long as they are fighting alongside the believers.
10. Medina shall remain sacred and inviolable for all that join this treaty.

11. Should any disagreement arise between the signatories to this treaty, then Allah, the All-High and His Messenger shall settle the dispute.
12. The signatories to this treaty shall boycott Quraish commercially, they shall also abstain from extending any support to them.
13. Each shall contribute to defending Madinah, in case of a foreign attack, in its respective area.
14. This treaty shall not hider either party from seeking lawful revenge.[4]

The ratification of the above treaty ultimately led to a coalition state with Holy Prophet as the President, Madinah proper as capital and with power mostly in the hands of Muslims. In order to extend the zone of peace the Prophet of Islam entered into similar treaties with other tribes living nearby.

RULER OF ISLAM'S RECONNAISSANCE MISSIONS

Having seen the unity between Helpers and the Emigrants and the Muslims and the non-Muslims of Arabs as well as Jews, the Quraish were terrified and were jealous of the rapidly growing influence of the Exalted Chief of Islam among the people of Medina and the surrounding areas. When it became difficult for them to tolerate, they decided to attack Muslims at their newly acquired place. However, before attacking they wanted to enlist the support of the non-Muslim tribes and the Jews living thereby. When the Quraish realized that there was opposition of Muslims from the sides of Jews they made clandestine contacts with 'Abdullah bin Uabi bin Salul, the chief of the polytheists of Medina and the president designate of the tribes of 'Aws and Khaztaj and asked him to expel the Honourable Prophet from Medina and not to cooperate with him failing which they threatened him to exterminate his people and proscribe his women. When the Mighty Hero of Islam came to know of the positive inclination of 'Abdullah bin Uabi bin Salul towards the Quraish of Makkah, he summoned him and admonished him. Consequently, he dropped the idea of helping the Quraish openly but heart to heart he was their sympathizer. Quraish finally sent a letter to the Muslims that they would soon attack them in their own homeland and liquidate all of them en masse. The Strategist Genius of Islam took this threat seriously and increased the security of his family and deputed soldiers on vital points to defeat enemy misadventures. He chalked out a most effective defence strategy to blunt the dirty intentions of his adversaries. The first thing that he did was that he sent reconnaissance patrols to explore the geopolitical features of roads and land routes surrounding Medina and leading to Makkah. He contacted the nearby tribes and tried to impress upon the polytheists and the Jews that Muslims were a power to reckon with and no one could attack them without facing the music. When the Holy Prophet came to know of several caravans after caravans of Meccans going to Syria passing along the shores of Red Sea, he realized the importance of enemy maneuvers and decided to check them. These caravans were not only providing enemies with huge amount of profits to fight wars against Muslims but they were also spreading hatred and misinformation among several tribes living in Syria and on route to Syria against Muslims. Moreover, the caravans had dangerous agents who were capable of sowing the seeds of discontent and dissentions among the people of Medina and enlist their support against the Muslims. Over and above this, if they were checked by force, a healthy signal was bound to go to the enemy that Muslims could not be taken for a ride since they had gathered a mighty force. The Magnificent Guide of Islam, therefore, sent small parties with a view to making the Meccans realize the formidable presence of Muslims in the area.

ARMED INVASIONS TO CHECK ENEMY MOVEMENTS

He sent a platoon named Saif Al-Bahr consisting of thirty Emigrants in 623 A.D. under Hamzah bin Abdul Muttalib for intercepting the caravans belonging to Quraish. They confronted the caravan of Quraish with three hundred people including Abu Jahal bin Hisham but due to the mediation of a common friend named Majid bin 'Amr, the matter was pacified. It was on this day that the famous Ruler of Islam accredited the first white flag in the history of Islam and entrusted it to Kinaz bin Hussain Al-Ghanawi with a view to carry it. In April 623 A.D. another troop was dispatched under the command of Ubaidah bin A-Harith bin Al-Muttalib heading sixty horsemen of Emigrants to a place called Batn Rabegh where they met the caravan of Quraish consisting of two hundred men headed by Abu Sufyan. The arrow throwing took place for a while but there was no actual confrontation. However, two Muslims Al-Miqdad bin 'Amr Al-Bahrani and 'Utbah bin Ghazwan Al-Mazini managed to defect to the side of Muslims from the caravan of Abu Sufyan. Likewise, in May 623 A.D. a unit consisting of twenty horsemen was sent under the supervision of Sa'd bin Abi Waqqas but when they reached As-Kharrar after a five-day journey, the enemy had left a day earlier. The same year, that is, 623 A.D. His Excellency the Ruler of Islam marched on his first invasion with a white flag carried by Hamzah bin Abdul Muttalib heading seventy men mostly Emigrants to intercept a camel caravan belonging to Quraish but when he reached Waddan a place between Medina and Makkah, he confronted none. During this period he deemed it fit to enter into a non-aggression pact with 'Amr bin Makhshi Ad-Damari. The provisions of the pact were as follows:

> This is a document from Muhammad, the Messenger of Allah concerning Bani Damrah in which he established them safe and secure in their wealth and lives. They can expect support from the Muslims unless they oppose the religion of Allah. They are also expected to respond positively in case the Prophet sought their help.[5]

Similarly, in 623 A.D. he went on Buwat invasion at the head of two hundred companions to intercept the caravan of Quraish which consisted of two thousand five hundred camels with hundred Quraishites along with Omaiya bin Khalaf but the caravan had left off before he reached there. Karz bin Jabir heading a small group of the polytheists invaded the pastures of Medina in 623 A.D. and looted some animals. In retaliation to it the Chief of Islam started on Sufwan invasion heading seventy men in their pursuit and reached Sufwan but could not catch them. In the same way, he could not confront the caravan of Quraish when he moved on Dhil' Ushairah invasion in

November-December 623 A.D. with thirty camels and one hundred fifty to two hundred companions because they had already fled. In January, 624 A.D. Abdullah bin Jahsh Asadi was deputed with six camels and twelve Emigrants with a letter from the Ruler of Islam with the condition that he should read the letter after two days. When he did so, he found that he was directed to go to Naklah standing between Makkah and At-Ta'if and to intercept the caravan of Quraish and collect information about their motives. There he found a caravan loaded with raisins, food stuff and other material of substance accompanied by notable polytheists including 'Amr bin Al-Hadrami, 'Uthman and Naufal, sons of Abdullah bin Al-Mugheerah and others. Muslims initially hesitated to fight due to the month of Rajab since in that month the war was prohibited in Arabia. They finally engaged them in which 'Amr bin Al-Hadrami was shot dead, Al-Hakam was captured and Naufal fled. They brought the booty to Medina but the Guide of Islam disapproved their action due to the prevailing conventions of fighting wars in Arabia, The companions were pained too much due to their wrong decision but their worries were removed when the Lord permitted the Muslims to fight even in the prohibited months to those polytheists who never recognized their own true God. These intelligent maneuvers of the Steward of Islam frightened the Quraish. They were more than convinced that in due course of time the whole area falling on the route of Makkah to Syria via the Red Sea would come under the control of Muslims and they would starve them.

THE MAIN FEATURES OF ISLAMIC STATE

The fears and the predictions of the non-believers proved to be correct. Within merely ten years the Commander of Islam in a bloodless revolution succeeded in establishing one of the most powerful states unilaterally especially from a position when he was lonely, persecuted and helpless. He established such a righteous, humanistic, secular and progressive state that the world had never seen before. It was a state where sovereignty lied neither in the king nor in the people but in the Lord and the ruler or the king was just a trusty or a representative or a vicegerent. The main duty of the ruler was to endow humanity with righteous life and to purge its evils, inviting all sections of the society to what is right and forbidding what is wrong and seeking their obedience as well as consulting them in the affairs of the governance for their betterment in this world and hereafter. He created a state where everyone was shepherd unto another and responsible for the welfare of the fold. The state provided freedom of religion, worship, faith and belief system to every individual irrespective of his caste, creed, colour, religion, sex and place of birth. It was the duty of the state to protect the life, property, possessions, honour and rights of each individual living within the bounds of the state since Islam considered human rights as indefeasible and inalienable rights of man to protect his personality.

The Guide of Islam gave a' Universal Charter', at the time of his Fare-Well address, the glimpses of which can be seen in the Charter of the UNO. Islamic state comprehensively charted out the rights and the duties of the individuals, groups and the state for righteous, harmonious and peaceful living. It made it pertinent on the part of the state to provide social security to its subjects in such a way that no subject was left without care and necessities of life because everyone was believed to be the rightful owner in the property and treasury of the state. Liberty and equality were enshrined in Islamic Constitution and it was also implied that the state would not only provide equal opportunity to each individual but would also see to it that nobody was discriminated and he got what was due to him. If one looks at all the political theories propounded by various thinkers about the governance of the state from time to time one would be more than convinced that the theories and concepts which have been provided by the Guide of Islam are far superior to all those that have been given by Greek, Roman, Medieval, Renaissance, Enlightened and Modern thinkers. The Genius of Islam was far ahead of his times. His genius lied in the fact that he did not give merely the theories of state craft in black and white on the piece of paper but also put before the people the model of the state which had no parallel in matters of justice, piety, brotherhood and peaceful co-existence. The beauty of the Islamic state was that since the

Holy Qur'an did not define the nature, kind, type, form, shape and decree of Islamic state but based it on principles and consultations, it was relevant under all forms of governance beneficial to mankind. It was the fault of Muslims that after the fall of the state established by the Steward of Islam, they could not continue the same.

THE HOLISTIC APPROACH OF THE RULER OF ISLAM

The Guide of Islam not only established the state but also enriched it with appropriate economic, social, cultural, educational and moral systems. He designed an economic system which was devoid of exploitation and usury. It was based on justice, equality, progress and mutual benefits. He forbade interest and built the whole economic system on the just and equitable foundations of sharing profits and losses which was beneficial to all sections of the society. He established a secular society around Medina which was based on justice, equity, piety and good conscience. He gave a complete code of conduct which covered all the aspects of life.

The Holy Prophet also gave the educational system which was not only most effective for the development of human personality but it was also holistic in nature. It provided them knowledge content, taught them wisdom, developed their personalities, created in them moral, material and spiritual perceptions and made them enlightened human beings. Muslim scholars did research on various aspects of life in the light of knowledge provided by Holy Qur'an and Sunna. They shined on the academic firmament like glittering stars. The educational institutions of Islam were not merely the skill forming centers as modern technical institutes are. They were educational centers in true senses. They developed multidimensional aspects of human personality such as physical, mental, social, cultural, aesthetical, moral and spiritual. The Islamic institutes not only taught them the art of decent earnings but also made them educated and enlightened citizens.

The Steward of Islam also gave the mankind nice system of 'Dawa' that is inviting non-believers politely, courteously and patiently towards Islam. He never used force in converting people to Islam but convinced them about the usefulness of Islam. When the non-Muslims were fully convinced, they accepted Islam in multitude.

TREAMENT OF NON-MUSLIMS IN THE ISLAMIC STATE

The world knows that the Ruler of Medina had promulgated a written constitution for his state which was a confederacy between Muslims, Jews and other tribes. It was based on secular principles, human rights and mutual cooperation. It was the period when the Ruler of Medina had not conquered most part of Southern Arabia and had not become the Chief of Arabian Peninsula yet he had safeguarded the belief systems of Jews, Bedouins Pagans and other non-Muslims and provided them freedom to propagate their religion. However, when several territories were conquered and many kingdoms were subdued several non-Muslims came under his stewardship. They were ensured security of life, property, possessions, honour, dignity and were guaranteed freedom of religion, worship and adoration. Their churches, synagogues, monasteries and places of worship were made safe and secure and they were free to practice and propagate their religion. These non-Muslims were known as Dhimmi, means protected by God and the Prophet. By payment of "Jizyah" which was a nominal amount they were guaranteed state protection. Only adult males, hale and hearty, possessing means to pay such amount were asked to pay "Jizyah". Ladies, children, old, handicapped, poor and the religious preachers were immune from "Jizyah". Besides, they were not compelled to join jihad. However, those who were willing to participate in Jihad were exempted from "Jizyah", Holy Ruler himself said, "Beware, I shall myself be the complainant on the day of Resurrection, against him who wrongs a Dhimmi or lays on him a responsibility greater than he can bear or deprives him of anything that belongs to him."[6] The Guardian of Islam was so concerned about the safety of the innocent non-Muslims that a few moments before he left for his heavenly abode he declared, "A Muslim who kills a Dhimmi has not the slightest chance of catching even the dimmest smell of Heaven. Protect them, they are my Dhimmis."[7] Likewise, Caliph Umar also asserted, "To him who will be the Caliph after me, I command my wish and testament! The Dhimmis are protected of God and the Prophet (PBUH) respect the covenants entered into with them, and when necessary fight for their interests and do not place on them burden or responsibility which they cannot bear."[8] It is a fact that the general laws which applied upon Muslims were also applicable upon non-Muslims. The difference was only in matters of personal laws. The Muslim personal laws applied upon Muslims and the personal laws of non-Muslims applied to non-Muslims. The non-Muslims also enjoyed the judicial autonomy. They had their tribunals and their own judges to apply their special civil and penal laws. Holy Ruler had declared at the time of his Farewell Pilgrimage that all people were equal since they were created by God and they were the children of Adam and Eve. Arab had no precedence over non-Arab, so also white was not superior to black. Only those were good who were righteous, pious, just and truthful. Non-Muslims who were captured as war prisoners were also treated humanely. Likewise, in the wake of conquering any territory the non-Muslim men and women were given nice treatment. Many non-Muslims were appointed on high positions due to their competence and it was ensured that no discrimination was made between the citizens of the state on the basis of religion. History testifies to this fact that Jews of Medina were economically well off compared to many Muslims. The business, trade and orchards were in their hands and they were the money lenders. Similarly, the Bedouins, polytheists and other non-believers too had full freedom in carrying on business, trade, profession and vocation. They could move in any part of the country without any restrictions. They had complete liberty in matters of observance of their customs, traditions, ethos and religious practices. Their saints, men of eminence and chiefs were accorded respects and regards due to them. Their religious books, educational centers and religious places were completely safe and secure. The state never interfered in their patterns of diets, dress codes, conducts of lives and behaviour patterns. In a sense non-Muslims were better off in various matters compared to Muslims.

It is a fact that the Mercy upon mankind spent ten restless years in Medina during which he never got rest for a single day. He spent most of his time in producing a cohesive society based on fraternity and the state based on justice, equity, piety and good conscience. He loved all the segments of the society irrespective of their places of births, economic backgrounds and belief systems. He created a band of dedicated companions who believed in God's help and never bothered about the might of the adversaries. They were brave, bold, pious, God-fearing and exemplary in conduct who spread the message of Islam in far and wide. Despite being small in number they fought with the multitude and turned out to be triumphant. They loved the Ruler of Islam more than their lives, honour, properties, possessions and kith and kin. Besides, he also created such a love and affection among the Emigrants and the Helpers that their brotherhood displaced kinship. He united Muslims, Jews, Bedouins, polytheists and the non-believers and brought them on a common platform as equals. He laid the foundation of Islamic society on love, mercy, allegiance and struggle which left a mark on the annals of history. He was indeed a model of perfection and greatness. He gave his time, energy, money, material, youth, old age, possessions and riches to the humanity and took nothing in return. He struggled throughout his life for the betterment of mankind but raised his sword when his Islamic state and Islamic society were challenged by the polytheists. The battle cry rose, the blood flowed, he too was wounded but ultimately he remained victorious.

NOTES

1. Michael H. Hart, op. cit., p. 34.
2. Abdul Hameed Siddiqui, op. cit., p. 145.
3. *Ibid.*, p. 148.
4. Shafiur Rahman al-Mubarakpuri, op. cit., pp. 197-98.
5. *Ibid.*, p. 203.
6. Muhammad Muslehuddin. "Islam and its Political System". (Kitab Bhavan, New Delhi, 1999), p. 57.
7. *Ibid.*
8. *Ibid.*

4

The Main Battles Fought by the Majestic Ruler

Holy Prophet, being the Mercy upon whole mankind, was always a peace-loving person. He could never dream of bloodshed, strives, dissensions, conflicts and wars. He tolerated extreme types of persecution for about 13 years in Makkah at the hands of hostile Quraish but did not raise his sword even in self-defence. When people decided to kill him he left Makkah for Medina to avoid bloodshed. He never attacked any State, Territory, Country or Kingdom. The battles that he fought were really those that were imposed upon him. He led twenty-seven campaigns in person during the last ten years of his life, in nine of which there was tough fighting. The number of expeditions which he planned, managed and supervised but sent out under others' leaderships were thirty-eight. He fought nine battles in person in which the Battles of Badr, Uhud and Trench were main and others were skirmishes. The world is witness to the fact that he was least interested to become the Ruler of Islamic state since his main mission being the Last Prophet of God was to convey the message of Islam to humanity.

UNPROVOKED AND CONSTANT AGGRESSIONS OF THE ADVERSARIES

It were the adversaries of Islam who by their constant aggressions, wars and misadventures made him the virtual ruler of whole of Arabia within ten years. If they would have not attacked him he would have peacefully remained confined at Medina and his Kingdom would have not extended to the territories of his defeated enemies. By very nature the Prophet of Islam was peace loving and avoided every conflict. He had no ambition whatsoever to become a Monarch or Ruler. He led a simple life. The world has also seen that despite being the Mighty Chief of one of the biggest kingdoms of the world his ways of living remained simple as before. The humanity cannot provide any example of any thinker, philosopher, friend, leader, reformer, orator, warrior, conqueror, apostle, legislator and emperor who single handedly changed the world map in such a short time. He was a wonderful theorist, perfect planner, sound adviser, thoughtful organizer, best strategist and ideal Humanist. In those ten years he destroyed polytheism and idolatry from Arabia and introduced the worship of one true God, raised the status of women from the status of chattels to dignified human beings and provided them legal status equal to men, stopped the drunkenness among Arabs which had disgraced them since time immemorial and developed among them love for humanity and honesty and sincerity in dealing with mankind. He transformed the ignorant, quarrelsome and the blood thirsty tribe into people with strong belief system, compassionate hearts, large-hearted tolerance and thirsty for knowledge. He abolished the differences between Arabs and non-Arabs, blacks and whites, rich and poor, slaves and freemen and for the first time in world history the human brotherhood was made a fact and the principle of common law a reality.

History testifies that the earliest phase of the Guardian of Islam at Medina was full of troubles and discords. He never intended to quarrel with any segment of the society for he wanted the peaceful atmosphere to spread the message of Islam but the Quraish were bent upon to liquidate him. With a view to physically, mentally and emotionally disturb him, they started aggressive and violent persecution of those new converts to Islam who were left behind at Makkah. In the early stages of Islam, the Muslims were in minority and had suffered immensely at the hands of Makkans who sought to stop them from professing their new faith. They tried their best to persuade them to leave their newly acquired faith but in vain. Similarly, they sent delegations to the King of Abyssinia to return those Muslims who had migrated to his kingdom in order to seek his protection but the King of Abyssinia protected them and did not help them. Finally, they started clandestine treaties and contacts with polytheists of Medina and hedged plots to kill the leader of the Muslims. They did not leave him in peace even in the far off refuge at Medina 210 miles from Makkah as they wanted to destroy the plant of Islam at its budding stage. They tried to incite the whole of peninsula against the Leader of Islam but he made all efforts to avoid confrontations with the Quraish and kept low profile. However, when he realized that it was futile to expect any good from them who were bent upon destroying him and his mission, he planned a suitable strategy to fight the enemy. Provocations, skirmishes and confrontations on minor scales started taking place here and there between Muslims, Jews and the polytheists of Medina.

FIRST DECISIVE BATTLE OF ISLAM AT BADR

To counter the dangerous plans of the enemies of Islam the Commander of Islam thought out a comprehensive defence strategy which proved very effective in the long run. To begin with he started a reconnaissance plan to watch the movements of the Makkans and entered into alliances with the nearby tribes to confront them. By his carefully designed strategic plan he impressed upon the Jews as well as all the other polytheists, Bedouins and heterogeneous tribes living in the surrounding areas that Muslims were a hard nut to crack. He sent proactive military dispatches and reconnaissance patrols in search of Quraish who were bent upon committing military aggression upon Muslims. The Leader of Islam actually wanted to shake the faith of prominent Quraish leaders like Abu Jahal, Abu Sufyan and others who were most prominent behind the plans to finish Islam from the face of earth. When he came to know that Abu Sufyan went out towards Syria with an immense caravan in which all the important Quraish of Makkah had bought shares, he deputed his troops to confront him at Al-Ushairah but he escaped safely. When he was returning with loaded camels near Medina on his way back to Makkah with wealth amounting to 50 thousand gold Dinars and guarded by forty men, Holy Prophet marched with 313 men, eighty-three from the Emigrants and sixty-one belonging to Aws and the rest to Al Khazra.[1] By capturing the caravan Muslims not only wanted to send a shock wave throughout Arabian Peninsula but also improve their economic positions and shake the confidence of Makkans. Islamic forces tried to surround the caravan near the surroundings of Medina but could not succeed because the leader of the caravan left the main route and escaped through coast-line of Red Sea. Abu Sufyan sought the help of the Quraish by communicating them in horrible style through a camel-rider who arrived in a worn out state and shouted frantically that their caravan was most likely to be ambushed by the Muslims.

Annoyed by it whole Makkah led by its nobles and elders marched towards Medina on 17th March, 624 (18 Ramadan AH 2) with 1300 soldiers including 100 horsemen, 600 mailed soldiers and a large number of camels to attack the Muslims at Badr.[2] They wanted to punish the Muslims as well as prevent them from intercepting their caravans in future. When Quraish came to know that Abu Sufyan had succeeded in reaching Makkah they thought of going back to Makkah but on the insistence of Abou Jahal they decided to rest and enjoy for three nights in eating good food, drinking wine and reveling at Badr which was a centre of seasonal gathering in that part of Arabia. Besides, they also wanted to create fear in all Arabs about their strength and give the impression to Muslims that they were not afraid of them. Muslims too did not want to take any risk. They also wanted to communicate the enemy that Muslims were a force to reckon with. They too marched towards Badr. Muslims were certainly not in favour of confronting the enemy since they were not only unprepared but also ill-equipped. They had merely 313 men, 70 camels and 2 horses and Quraish had nearly 1000 soldiers at the time when they were enjoying at Badr since a few of them had already left the scene having heard about the safety of the caravan. However, when the two forces faced each other, the war became inevitable.

The sense of justice, equity, courage and farsightedness of the Leader of Islam can be judged by the fact that he did not persuade all who were with him to confront his mighty enemy but allowed all the Ansars, that is, the residents of Medina to return to their homes because their oath to fight along with him was confined only to Medina and not in the open fields. No man on earth would have done that having seen the strong enemy standing against him with its full might. If the people of Medina would have deserted him, he would have been left with eighty-three Emigrants only that too highly ill equipped to face well-prepared strong force of one thousand enemy soldiers. Since he did not want to violate the terms of treaty even under highly odd circumstances, he took the greatest risk of his life and allowed them to go to their homes. The world is amazed till date why the Commander of Islam bothered so much for the terms of treaty when his own life and the survival of his religion was in danger. It is only when we see such impossible things happening in the lives of Great men that we begin to say that indeed they were different people. Thanks to the Ansars that they firmly stood like rock with the Prophet and assured him to sacrifice their last drop of blood for his safety and security.

Fortified by the help of God and the assurances of his faithful, Holy Prophet himself commanded them as their Commander-in-Chief. History knows that when he was at the Head of the Command, he did not take unilateral decisions but involved his colleagues. He consulted his companions practically on all matters pertaining to chalking out the action plans, gathering of intelligence as well as adopting the suitable strategies. He did not command his forces from behind or through remote controls but led them from front. He went alone on reconnaissance missions and questioned the secret agents himself which no Commander-in-Chief would have done so under those circumstances. The war strategists are astonished how with the strategic management of such a meager ill-equipped force he succeeded in smashing the enemy in no time. He analyzed the strengths and weaknesses of his forces before planting them on battle fields. He also selected suitable commanders to lead the small units keeping in mind their bravery, acumen and dexterity. Finally, he divided the army in small formations with separate commanders having their white standards and asked them not to attack the enemy unless the enemy compelled them to fight. The enemies of Islam also saw that he never allowed his passion for peace and harmony to desert him even at the wake of strongest provocation by telling his troops not to start the war till it was imposed upon them. The Islamic forces were highly motivated. They were preceded by two black flags and marched as the iron wall and fought bravely with the help of God. There were ups and downs in the war. Many a time the Islamic units did wonders and many a time the Leader of Islamic forces reached to the position where it appeared to him that enemy was at the verge to over-rule them and wipe out Islam from the face of the globe but he did not leave hope. He believed in His Almighty God, encouraged his forces, supported and guided them through the thick and thin and the ultimate result was astonishing. The first to be killed was Al-Aswad bin Abdul Asad Al-Makhzumi, a worst, bad tempered and a fierce person. The battle first went against the ill-equipped Muslims but ended into a miraculous victory for Muslims. The enemy was defeated and the Muslims turned out to be the conquerors. Historians and war strategists are wonderstruck how an untrained, ill-equipped and meek army defeated the might of the well fortified, strong and experienced enemy force. Here one has to say that God was certainly with the Leader of Islam because without His help he could not accomplish his task of liquidating his adversaries who were mightier than him practically in all spheres.

It will not be out of place to mention here that it was the first defensive war against the enemies of Islam in which the Holy Prophet himself took part and in which the causalities were minimal. Only fourteen Muslims were killed out of which six were from Emigrants and eight from the helpers. As against this merely seventy adversaries were killed and nearly equal numbers were taken as prisoners.[3] Those who levy the charge on the Holy Prophet of spreading Islam by the sword should know that as early as 281 B.C. when Asoka conquered Kalinga nearly one hundred thousand persons were killed and even a larger number were injured. Likewise, it is claimed that 500,000 French soldiers died during the Napoleonic war and 8,000,000 Germans were killed during the Second World War.

Moreover, the Prophet of Islam did not follow the brutal ethics of Pre-Islamic days when the captives were mostly humiliated, tortured and butchered but treated them nicely. He ordered the killing of only two prisoners of wars namely, An-Nadr bin Al-Harith and Uqbah bin Abi Muait who were hardened criminals and who according to modern practice should have been awarded death penalty. They had not only persecuted Muslims at Makkah beyond limits but were the main planners and whose killing was to be communicated as a stern warning to the adversaries of Islam. He asked his followers to treat rest of them well by feeding nicely and behaving humanely. He distributed the captives among his companions. Some of them were freed after paying ransom according to their financial positions, a few were released in exchange of Muslim captives and those who could not pay the money were set free when each one of them taught ten children the art of writing and reading. Some of them were freed even without paying the ransom on compassionate grounds. Over and above this, Holy Prophet did not keep all the booty of War to himself but kept one fifth portion with him to be used in the name of God for poor, destitute and those whom he deemed fit and the rest he distributed equally among participants. He also behaved graciously with those who were dead and did not mutilate their bodies as the Quraish did after the battle of Uhud. After the battle of Uhud some of the Quraish and their women mutilated the bodies of the dead Muslim soldiers. Many of them cut off their genitals and bellies and defaced them by cutting their noses and ears and dishonouring their bodies. Hind bin Utbah, the wife of Abu Sufyan ripped open the liver of Hamzah and chewed it. She even made the anklets and necklaces of the chopped ears and noses.

AFTEREFFECTS OF BADR

The Battle of Badr had not only broken the backbone of Quraish but it had also shattered the Jews of Medina and the polytheists of nearby areas. Quraish were burning in revenge and the Jews were finding it difficult to see the rising clout of the Prophet in Medina. They became more serious and started planning against Muslims despite a covenant between them. They resorted to spying, divisive poetry, rumour mongering and hate campaigns. It appeared as if the scene of war had reverted to Medina instead of Makkah. The hatred between Jews and Muslims multiplied day by day. Holy Prophet was keeping a close watch over all the developments. Meanwhile a few important developments took place. Muslims were very bitter of the aggressive attitudes of a few adversaries of Islam especially Abu Afk, a tribe man of Bani Amr bin Awf and Asma daughter of Marwan belonging to the tribe of Bani Umayyah Zayd who used to write defamatory poetries against Muslims and Holy Prophet and insult Islam and the Prophet of Islam. One day Saleem bin Umayr killed both of them. To Abu Afk he caught and killed him then and there. Likewise, he attacked Asma and liquidated her boldly and courageously. Likewise, Ka'b bin Al Ashraf too was killed for defaming Islam and the Holy Prophet. Ka'b's father was an Arab and belonged to the tribe of Tayy but his mother was a Jewess from the tribe of Bani Nadir. He was a rich and famous man. He used to write poetries against Muslims and Islam. He went to Makkah and wrote poetries in favour of the nobles of Quraish and incited them to attack Muslims. Many young Muslims were so irritated that they decided to finish Ka'b bin Al Ashraf at any cost. They asked Abu Na'ilah to go in search of him and kill him at the earliest opportunity. Na'ilah intelligently got his confidence and one day finding opportune time killed him and relieved the agony of many Muslims who were very bitter to him. In grief and indignation the Jews of Bani Nadir approached the Prophet and complained him about the killing of Ka'b. Holy Prophet reminded them about his nefarious activities which were against the covenant signed between

Muslims and Jews. He advised them to enter into a special treaty which they willingly agreed.

THE BATTLE OF UHUD

Quraish were bewildered by the defeat at Badr and wanted to take revenge as early as possible. They took the support of the well-known tribes like Kinana and Tihamah as well as the Bedouins of Ahabish. They also decided to use the profit of the escaped caravan of Abu Sufyan amounting to 1000 camels and fifty thousand Dinars for the purchase of the war equipments. They also hired poets for enticing the tribes and took their women with them so that they might arouse them to fight the adversaries. They moved under Abu Sufyan with their three thousand fierce warriors, of which seven hundred were well-armoured men and two hundred well-mounted cavalry, three thousand camels and fifteen women. The general command of the army was under the over all control of Abu Sufyan who was in the central position, the right wing with hundred horses was commanded by Khalid bin Al Walid, and the left with the same number of horses by Ikrimaf bin Abou Jahl and Safwan bin Omaiya was in-charge of infantrymen. Al-Abbas bin Abdul Muttalib sent the message regarding the movement of the army of Quraish which the Holy Prophet got at Quba Mosque. He immediately started consultations. Prophet's initial idea was to defend the city of Medina as suggested by Abdullah ibn Ubeyy but it was opposed by a majority of people. Finally, it was decided that the enemy should be confronted at Mount Uhud. The Prophet of Islam moved with one thousand soldiers out of which one hundred were armoured and fifty were horsemen. He divided the army into three battalions. Mus'ab bin Ummair As-Abdari commanded the Al-Muhajireen battalion, Usaid bin Hudair the Al Ansari-Aws battalion and Al-Hubab bin Al-Mundhir the Al-Ansari-Khazraj battalion. When the enemy reached the destination Abdullah bin Ubai, the hypocrite under a well thought out plan to weaken the Muslims rebelled and withdrew with his three hundred men from the scene of war. Thus, Muslims were left merely with seven hundred soldiers. The foe also tried to create further dissension among the ranks and files of Muslims by enticing them, offering several charms but they could not succeed.

The genius of the Prophet of Islam devised a foolproof plan of War. Although he had approached the Site of war later than his adversaries, he managed to select most favourable position under the given circumstances. He chose the high place for encampment from where he could inflict maximum causalities to enemy forces fighting on the lower ridges. He used the rocky mountain of Uhud as the shield for the army's rear and right flank and blocked the only vulnerable gap on the side and provided maximum protection for the rear as well as the left wing. He also provided additional safe guards to Muslims in the wake of fleeing for fear of defeat and falling prey to the enemy by encamping them on high position. As a matter of fact he left no choice for the enemy save facing Muslims from the narrow place in the lower region. If they tried to capture the position of Muslims or dared to approach them they were bound to suffer heaviest loss. Moreover, he arranged the forces into two rows and deputed fifty expert archers on the side of the mountain under the command of Abdullah bin Jubair. He instructed Al-Zubyr bin Al-Awam to confront Khalid bin Walid with his forces and ordered other group to face the cavalry of the adversaries. He issued orders to the fighters to stay wherever they were. He directed them to drive off the enemy horses from Muslims by means of arrows if they dared to come towards them or attack the Islamic forces from behind. He asked them to make it sure that in no case Muslims were attacked from their sides and told them not to leave their places irrespective of the fact whether the Muslims won or lost. They were not to leave their positions even if Muslims were snatched into pieces by birds without his permission. He also told them not to come to their rescue even if they were slain and not to come to them if they were winning or gaining ground till they heard from him but to remain steadfast under all circumstances and see to it that they were not attacked from their sides.[4] Thus, by deputing the squad on the mountainside, Holy Prophet tried his best to block the only groove that might lead the enemy to attack from behind and encircle the Muslims from all sides. He appointed al-Mundhir bin Amron on the right wing, Az-zubair bin Al-Awwam on the left and deputed Al-Miqbad bin Al-Aswaf his Assistant and supporter. He specifically advised Az-Zubair to confront effectively the horsemen of Khalid bin Walid.

He ordered them not to fight without orders from him. The enemy poets started to inflame the emotions of the troops and their women wandered among the rows of enemy soldiers encouraging them to fight. The two forces came nearer and nearer to each other. The combat started in March, 625 (7 Shawwal AH 3) with standard bearer of the enemy Talha bin Abi Talha Al-Abdari riding on his camel and challenging the Muslims to fight. Az-Zubair bin Al-Awwam advanced and killed the rogue. Soon the general engagement took place and both the armies fiercely clashed with each other. Prophet's strategy especially in planting archers under the command of Abd Allah bin Jubair paid dividend. The archers located on Archers mountain defeated the efforts of Khalid bin Walid supported by Abu Amir Al Fasiq when they tried thrice to enter through left and create confusion in the rear portion of the Muslim army. The skilled archers kept the Meccan horses at bay. Enemies could not dare to confront Muslims from any corner and many of them were killed and Muslims got their upper hand. Unfortunately Hamzah bin Abdul Muttalib was martyred by the spear of Washi bin Harb who treacherously threw it from behind the tree. Washi was the slave of Jubair bin Mut'im. He was assigned the task at the behest of Hinda in return of huge wealth and by his master Tuaimah whose uncle Tu'aimah bin Adi was injured at Badr in lieu of freeing him. Muslims fought like hungry lions and over powered enemy ranks. Having seen their defeat and the upper hand of Muslims, the Quraish ran in search of their lives forgetting their honour, promises, pride and dignity. Their standards were trodden by the feet of the fleeing enemies and there was none to protect them. Likewise, Hind bin 'Utba, her friends and servants were running with their garments gathered up. They were fleeing in the mountain with their ankles and legs revealed and their idols that they had carried had fallen on the grounds and broke in thousands of pieces. Muslims followed the enemies far from the battle field and those who remained behind collected the spoils of the fleeing forces. Ironically many Muslims abandoned pursuing the defeated soldiers and involved themselves in collecting the war booty. When the small portion of Muslim army was recording their memorable second victory, the majority of archers committed a fatal mistake which not only changed the whole situation upside down but caused immense loss of lives, and almost brought about the martyrdom of the Holy Prophet and left a permanent scar on the face of Islamic history. Despite the strict orders not to leave their positions at any cost, most of the archers deserted their posts and involved themselves in collecting the spoils of war save nine brave archers and their leader. Abdullah bin Jubair reminded them about the instructions of the Holy Prophet and reminded them of the consequences of deserting the strategic location but nobody paid any heed to it. Khalid bin Walid considered it a golden opportunity and he entered from the rear, killing Jubair and his nine supporters and seized the strategic mountain-side where Muslim archers were located. Muslims were bewitched between two enemy forces. Confusion mounted in Islamic forces to such an extent that some of them were killed by their own people by mistake.

Holy Prophet along with his nine supporters was surrounded by the enemy in the rear portion. He was attacked by all sides and severely wounded and a cry rose that he was slain, till someone recognized him and shouted that he was still alive. Many Muslims had lost hearts after hearing the demise of the Holy Prophet but they rallied after the shout. The Prophet of Islam without caring for his life stood courageously and boldly called his companions to fight with their all might without caring for the danger which he was inviting by exposing his critical location. The courage, bravery and power of the Commander of Islam can be judged by the fact that not only he fought alone facing all the might of the enemy but also did not conceal his position which strategists normally do under such circumstances. He not only motivated his soldiers to fight but also reminded his adversaries that he was alive and not dead as they had presumed. When the adversaries came to know of his presence in a precarious position, they moved en mass towards him even before the Muslims could reach him. Many weak-hearted and peripheral in belief system left the scene of war. Some of them reached as far as Medina, a few moved towards the mountain side and the rest sought refuge in nearby areas. Those who were slightly stronger in faith moved towards Holy Prophet but were entrenched in such a situation that they could not distinguish between enemies and friends and suffered immensely. The adversaries were successful to a great extent in demoralizing many weak hearted Muslims by spreading the rumour of his demise. This had jolted them heavily and their moral went down and many of them stopped fighting and some of them even met Abdullah bin Ubai, the head of the polytheists with a view to seek security pledge from Abu Sufyan. The last group consisting of Abu Bakr, Ummar bin Al-Khattab, Ali bin Abi Talib and others were strongest in faith, belief and commitment and cared for nothing but for the safety of the Holy Prophet. Messenger of the God was confined to a trap along with his seven Helpers and two Emigrants when the enemy soldiers attacked him. His companions received the blows of enemy arrows and suffered from the wounds of enemy swords but protected him till seven of them were killed. Finally, Holy Prophet was left with merely the two defenders namely Talha bin Ubaidullah and Sa'd bin Abi Waqqas who defended him to the last. One of the stones pelted by Utbah bin Abi Waqqas fell on the face of the Prophet of Islam and wounded his lower lip and knocked him to the ground. His lower incisor, that is, the tooth between a canine and front tooth was injured.[5] Abdulah bin Shihab Az-Zuhri also attacked the Holy Prophet on his shoulder with his sword, cleaving his forehead and causing the two rings of his iron-ringed helmet to penetrate in his cheek. Holy Prophet did not bother about these trifles but fought bravely dampening the morale of the enemy. It is told that Genghis Khan, Alexander and Cyrus used to fight along with their patriots in the front lines but hardly anyone of them fought lonely surrounded by their dreaded adversaries and that too addressing their mighty opponents publicly. Besides, his greatness lies in the fact that he did not curse his enemies in the wake of his injury but prayed God by saying "O Allah, forgive my people for they have no knowledge." When Muslims heard the voice of the Holy Prophet, they were convinced that he was alive. They moved towards him encircling him like a protective wall. Their faith was renewed and they jumped upon the enemies like the hungry lions. Holy Prophet withdrew up to the cover of the mountain and commanded the Muslims from there. When the Quraish knew that the Messenger of God was alive they thought it better to flee considering themselves as the victorious. Hind, daughter of Utbah took her women comrades onto the battle field and started mutilating the dead Muslims. She amputated a number of noses and ears to make necklace of them. She even cut open the body of Hamzah and pulled out his liver and chewed it.[6] Holy Prophet was shocked and broken having seen the fate of Hamzah and the mutilated bodies of the Muslims. He asked the Muslims to treat the dead of the enemies with utmost regard and ordered the seventy to be buried and when this was over, he headed towards Medina.

Those who blame the Prophet of Islam of bloodshed should know that in retaliation of 3000 dead and worth 10 billion dollar property loss on 9/11 September, the United States of America killed officially 6 hundred thousands and un officially 2 million Iraqis and nearly two hundred thousand Afghanis including innocent children, women, aged, sick and disabled civilians but as against this Muslims suffered merely the casualties of seventy people in all at the battle of Uhud which they fought in their self-defence.[7] Though The Commander of Islam had got an adverse set back and was wounded badly but he did not sit ideal. He followed the offensive strategy of chasing the enemies. He knew that the jerk at Uhud was bound to have an adverse affect upon the fate of the Muslims. They were bound to be looked down by the hypocrites, Jews and the polytheists of Medina as well as by the fellows of Abd Allah bin Salul who had not participated at the aforesaid battle. Besides, there were many non-believing tribes and clans who were not happy with the emergence of Muslims near and around Yathrib. He, therefore, decided to be proactive and deputed a unit to follow and pursue the enemy to a reasonable extent so that it could create a fear in the minds of the adversaries of Islam in and around Medina that Muslims were not subdued and side by side it could deter the Meccans to revert back. Thanks to his strategy as well as to the friendly behaviour of Bedwi who met Abu Sufyan and convinced him that Muslims were in the field and they were stronger than ever and thirsting for revenge, Abu Sufyan decided to move towards Makkah and left the scene of war.

AFTERSHOCKS OF UHUD

The reverse suffered at Mount Uhud affected the morale as well as the credibility and the reputation of Muslims adversely. Muslims prestige and power lowered down in the eyes of the people. Troubles and dangers spread everywhere near and around Medina. The enemies of Islam started talking openly about the precarious conditions of Muslims and efforts were made by the rival forces to liquidate the Muslims en mass. Though Quraish did not succeed in wiping out Islam from the map of the world but they surely accomplished the task of taking revenge of Badr from Muslims. The apparent defeat at Uhud encouraged the hypocrites of Medina to antagonize and disturb Holy Prophet and his followers. Muslims became an attractive and easy target of Jews, Bedouins and local tribes. Prophet knew that he had actually lost his military credibility at Mount Uhud but he wisely used all his meager resources intelligently. He managed to keep all the adverse forces at a safe distance and succeeded in regaining his power and prestige within no time. He took pro active steps by sending military missions, pursuing the enemies and defeating them on their own grounds. In no time he turned the whole table in favour of Muslims who were feeling helpless and neglected. He reemerged on the scene with such a flying colours that the adversaries of Islam were left spell bound and confounded.

Merely two months had passed after this battle that Holy Prophet was informed that the sons of Khuwaylid and leaders of Bani Asad were planning to attack Medina. He dispatched a strong force of hundred and fifty fighters under the command of Abu Salamah bin Abdl Asad but the enemy fled. Muslims pursued them and caught them by surprise and stripped them of their cattle, homeland and possessions. Likewise, when the Prophet heard that Khalid bin Suffian bin Nubayh was inciting people to march towards Medina, he ordered Abd Allah bin Unays to find his whereabouts. Abdullah finally succeeded in killing him. A few days back a tribe came to Holy Prophet and requested him to send some of his companions to teach Islam to them. Following the covenant of Aqabah, he sent six and in another version ten of his eminent companions with them. When they reached a Place known as Ar-Raji situated between Rabigh and Jeddah, they were attacked by hundred archers of Banu Lihyan clan. Muslims took shelter on a high mountain but despite the fact they were assured by Fudfud and the Bedouins that they would not be killed, three of them were killed on the spot and one while moving towards Makkah. The two of them Khubayb of Aws and Zayd of Khazraj were sold by Hudhayl at Makkah and they were killed mercilessly by their captors for killing some notables at Badr. Khubaib was crucified and Safwan bin Omaiyah killed Zaid bin Ad Dalhna for killing his father.

In a more or less similar situation the Ma'una Well tragedy took place in the same month which was more tragic than Ar-Raji. Abu Bara came to Holy Prophet and requested him to send few of his learned colleagues to Najd to teach Islam to his tribe. Prophet was most reluctant due to Ar-Raji episode and expressed his fear that the people of Najd might kill them. However, on the specific assurance of their safety and security by Abu Bara Amir bin Malik who was the Chief of Amir he sent his beloved forty or according to another version seventy companions to Najd. Unfortunately, his nephew plotted against him and the people of Usaiyah, Ri,al and Dhakwan who were folk of Bani Saleem surrounded them treacherously and thirty-nine of them were martyred while fighting gallantly save Ka'b bin Zaid bin An-Najjar who was brought wounded from among the dead. It is the irony of fate that the adversaries of Islam painted the killing of two hardened criminals by the Muslims after the battle of Badr as an atrocious act but they kept mum on the treacherous killing of many companions of the Holy

Prophet by his enemies against all the cannons of justice, equity and good conscience.

The events of treacherously killing Muslims by the adversaries of Islam surely and certainly lowered the prestige of Muslims in the eyes of the nearby tribes of Arabs as well as the Jews of Madinah. Jews despite their treaty with Muslims began to side openly with the Quraish of Makkah. Those Tribes such as Bedouins and Jews who were inclined to Muslims shifted their loyalties towards Quraish. Muslims began to be attacked by the rivals wherever they visited in small number. The Jews and the hypocrites of Medina took the opportunity to incite the Quraish and the enemies of Islam to attack upon Medina with a view to wipe out Islam from the scene. Holy Prophet realized the sensitivity of the situation and approached the Jews of Bani Al Nadir at Quba who were the allies of Bani Amir and asked them to cooperate in raising the blood money for two persons who were killed mistakenly by Amir bin Umayyah. Prophet of Islam soon realized that their intentions were not good. They were talking of the murder of Ka'b bin Al-Ashraf by the Muslims and planning to assassinate the Holy Prophet. Amir bin Jahsh had volunteered to drop a large millstone on his head but he was persuaded by Saleem bin Mashkam not to commit the folly. Holy Prophet tactfully left the scene and communicated Banu Nadeer through Mohammad bin Maslamah that the plot to kill him was in violation to the covenant which was given to them by him hence they were given ten days to leave the area after which they would be dealt with firmly. Abdullah bin Ubai asked the Jews not to leave their home land and assured them of the help of his two thousand supporters and the meaningful help from Quraizah tribe and Banu Ghatfan. Jewish leader Huyayy bin Akhtab replied that they would not leave the place and fight to the last.

Muslims confronted the situation of what to do and what not to do for if they attacked the Jews, they were likely to face fierce resistance and if they kept mum the enemies of Islam were bound to become more aggressive. Muslims had suffered at Uhud and they were certainly weak militarily and strategically. They had no allies to fall back upon and were surrounded everywhere by their enemies. Moreover, the Bani

An-Nadeer too was a strong tribe. It had its allies among the Quraish and other neighbouring fearful tribes. Thus opening a new front was disastrous from every angle. On the other hand, Khubeyb one of the envoys of Prophet was captured by one of the desert tribes and sold to Quraish who executed him publicly. Muslim delegations were being attacked openly, the Jews of Medina and the Bedouins and the hypocrites of nearby areas were plotting openly. They had even planned to kill the Prophet of Islam.

Under such circumstances the qualities of leadership demanded a bold and decisive step which the Holy Prophet took. It was in August 625 A.D. that Muslim cornered the Jews for six, fifteen or twenty days and twenty nights and battled ferociously. Jews waited for the help from bin Ubayy and other tribes and when Quraizah became neutral and the Ghatfan tribe did not help, they became frustrated. As they were situated and fortified comfortably and their thick palm trees provided them protection, they fought bravely but ultimately could not match the strategy of the Muslims. The siege did not last long and their leader Huyayy bin Akhtab approached the Holy Prophet with trembling hands and asked him to guarantee their lives and properties and provide them safe passage. The Commander of Islam should not have shown mercy upon the people of Banu Nadeer who had made his life hell especially at that time when he was facing one of the worst periods of his life but being the Mercy upon mankind he allowed each one of them to carry three camel loads of whatever property or goods they wanted to take or as much as their camels could lift except arms. Their caravan with six hundred loaded camels moved towards Khyber and Syria. They left behind their lands, houses, and wealth including fifty pieces of armours, fifty helmets, three hundred and forty swords, and large stretches of lands which were mainly distributed among the emigrants from Makkah. It relieved the burden of Ansars to a great extent. The strategic victory of Muslims over Bani An-Nadeer established the undisputed control of Muslims over Medina. Jews of Medina were the constant source of trouble and the disguised and open enemies of Muslims. Their continued presence in the city posed a constant threat or incitement or civil unrest and it was in the interest of Muslims to keep them at bay. Holy Prophet got sufficient time to crush those nearby fierce desert tribes that were treacherously killing Muslims missions and plotting against them day and night.

Muslims were very happy because the Jews had left the city and their properties and possessions had helped them immensely. However, on the anniversary of Uhud, Prophet recalled Abu Sufyan's pledge to meet at Badr after one year. Abu Sufyan sent Nu'aym to Madinah to inform the Muslims that Quraish had assembled a vast and magnificent army never seen before and the Meccans were preparing to fight them at Badr. Many Muslims were terrified and several of them lost courage. Thereupon Holy Prophet told them that if nobody accompanied him he alone would go and fight the enemy. History cannot sight a single example when the Commander of an armed force found his soldiers hopelessly shaken but he did not lose hope. He stood firm like a mountain and dared to confront his mightiest and most powerful adversaries single handedly. The Prophet's anger brought them to senses and they mustered courage, collected their weapons and rallied with the Prophet. Holy Prophet marched in 626 A.D. along with one thousand and five hundred warriors and ten mounted horsemen and reached Badr. Abu Sufyan too set out to fight with two thousand footmen and fifty horsemen and stopped at Mar Az-Zahran some distance from Makkah. He was so terrified that he could not dare to face the Holy Prophet. He advised his colleagues to return to Makkah and not to face the enemy as it was their drought year. The fearful retreat of Abu Sufyan not only diminished any future chances of war with Muslims in near future but also humiliated Quraish as much as they were humbled after the defeat of Badr. Muslims waited for eight days at Badr did wonderful business and enjoyed Lords Grace. When Abu Sufyan returned to Makkah and people found the polytheists, hypocrites and the idolaters virtually surrendered before Holy Prophet, the balance of power shifted in favour of Muslims. They regained their past glory and dignity and emerged as undisputed power in whole of the area.

When Muslims returned Medina they were very happy because Quraish who were their dead enemies had developed fear of Muslims in their hearts. While they were in a holiday mood information came to the Holy Prophet that a group from Ghatafan in the Najd were plotting an attack against them. Holy Prophet dispatched a strong force of four hundred soldiers for effective attack upon Dhat Al-Riqa where the Bani Muharib and Bani Tha'labah of Ghatafan had assembled. The enemy could not face Muslims might and fled leaving behind their women, equipments and possessions. Muslims brought as much as they could carry and remained alert for any surprise attack by the side of the enemy as a retaliatory measure but the adversaries could not muster support and Muslims prestige further enhanced in the region.

Likewise, when it was told to the Prophet that some tribes nearby Doumat Al-Jandal on the borders of Syria were planning to attack Medina he moved with one thousand fighters. Since he wanted to protect himself from enemy he used to move in the night to divert enemy attention. When he came near the spot, he was told that the inhabitants of Doumat Al-Jandal and the plotters had left leaving their cattle and shepherds. Holy Prophet stayed for five days and tried his best to capture them but in vain. Thus, with his far sight, better strategy, efficient planning and genius, Holy Commander of Islam was able to secure peace, progress and prosperity for the people of Medina and the surrounding areas. Most of the Jews had left the place and those who were there could not dare to challenge or harm the Muslims. Similarly, the Bedouins, hypocrites, polytheists and idolaters too had disintegrated and could not think for a moment to dent Muslims. Muslims took the advantage of the peaceful situation since there was no internal or external challenge to them in matters of spreading the message of Islam.

THE CAMPAIGN OF THE TRENCH (AL KHANDAQ)

Quraish of Makkah were not fully satisfied with the outcome of the battle of Uhud. They wanted to bring down Muslims to their knees. Likewise, the Jews of Medina and the Bedouin tribes of the surrounding areas too were bitter. They had suffered too much at the hands of Muslims. Moved by a common cause of eliminating Muslims from the Arabian Peninsula, they devised a strategy to attack Muslims with forming a combined force consisting of Quraish, Jews and the Bedouins. Twenty chiefs of Jews along with the nobles of Bani Nadir and Huvay and other Jewish leaders of Khaybar approached the Quraish at Makkah and assured them of their help and assistance. The Jews assured them to take the support of all the nomads of Najd in favour of them. The same delegation contacted the Bani Asad and Bani Ghatafan tribe and prepared them for the task. They toured most part of Arabia and formed a confederation of the non-believers against the Holy Ruler of Islam. Quraish, Kinnah and their allies from Tihama under the leadership of Abu Sufyan recruited four thousand men. The Gatafanite clans of Fazarah, Murrah and Ashja contributed two thousand soldiers and Bani Sulayman helped by sending seven hundred fighters. They all assembled at Makkah and formed a strong force of ten thousand fighters. Their number was more than the combined strength of Muslims at Medina including children and women. They were enough to exterminate Muslims en mass. They had three hundred horsemen and the Ghatafan had assured of similar number from Makkah. When the brave and courageous Commander came to know of it, he called a consultative meeting with a view to devise a suitable strategy. On the advice of Salman Al-Farsi, it was finally agreed to dig trenches around Medina to defend the town. They needed to dig trenches only where the protection of houses and masses of rocks and mountains were not available. Pickaxes, shovels, mattocks and baskets to carry excavated earth were borrowed from Bani Qurayyzah which they readily provided in view of common danger. Holy Ruler divided the task among his companions making each supervisor responsible for completing the work in due course of time with himself as their overall in-charge. Dressed in his red cloak, breast covered with dust, black hair touching shoulders, he worked with Emigrants as well as Helpers sometimes with a pickaxe, sometimes with a shovel and sometimes with a basket. Muslims with the constant hard work and extreme devotion of their colleagues achieved their target despite facing several problems including severe hunger bordering starvation. Holy Commander too took active part in digging and bore the brunt of extreme hunger.[8] Humanity can hardly show any case when a Magnificent Ruler worked along with his people as an ordinary labourer working hard day and night without food. Hardly they had finished their task in six days that they came to know that the Quraish army was advancing down the valley of Aqiq and it was near the south west of the town and the Ghatafan and other tribes of Najd were approaching Uhud from the east. All the houses facing battle lines were evacuated and the inhabitants were moved in safer areas. Holy Ruler camped with his red leather tent and three thousand fighters at the foot of Mount Sal.

The Guide of Islam had chosen such a wonderful strategic position that left the enemy to settle at a less advantageous position. Quraish and their allies established their camps separately near Mount Uhud. The Quraish were puzzled to see that their camels shall have to survive merely on the acacias of the valley of Aqiq and the camels of Ghatafan on the two varieties of tamarisk which grow near Uhud since the produce of the oasis had already been gathered. However, for the horses of both the units there was nothing to eat. It was, therefore, in their interest to finish the ask as early as possible. Abu Sufyan was the commander in-chief, Khalid and Ikrimah bin Abu Jahal were leading the Makkan cavalry and Amr was accompanying Khalid. As soon as the Makkan cavalry moved towards Medina they were frustrated having seen the trench before them which their horses could not cross. Over and above this, they were in the reach of the archers of the enemy who were ever ready to confront them. They thought it better to retreat to the safe place. They decided that a group of fighters commanded by Amr bin 'Abd-e-Wudud, Lkrima bin Abi Jahl and Dirar bin Al-Khatttab should pass through the trench. They partly succeed in capturing a marshy area between the trench and Sila mountain. However, in the dual Amr was killed by Ali bin Abi Talib and the enemy fled in confusion. Thank to the trench that no direct engagement took place between the rivals save the few encounters here and there.

Having seen Muslims in a strong position the Chief of Bani Nadir Huyai chalked out a strategy. He approached Ka'b bin Asaf Al-Qurazi to seek his help against Muslims who had a peace treaty with the Prophet. When he was told that Quraish and Al-Asyal and Ghatafan as well as other chiefs were bent upon destroying Muslims he agreed to violate the treaty. Bani Quraiza started war against Muslims especially in the secluded garrison that housed the women and the children of Muslims. One of the Jews actually managed to reach there but he was killed by Safiyah bint Abdul Muttalib which terrorized the Jews and they never dared to attack again. When the Commander of Islamic forces came to know of it he sent some fighters to Medina to protect the women and children. Holy Prophet tried his best to make peace with Ghatafan tribes and others but failed miserably. Finally Muslims too used Nu'am who set various segments of enemy such as Quraish, Ghatafan, Bani Quraiza and other Bedouin tribes at odds with each other. A confusion and mistrust arose among enemy ranks and files and they hesitated to act decisively. Moreover, a bitter and fierce wind blew for three days and nights from the sea which uprooted all the tents. The weather was so terribly cold, wet and fierce that neither the fire lighted nor a pot boiled and it was accompanied by torrents of rain which compelled people to seek shelter in safe areas.[9] Abu Sufyan finally decided to retreat crying that his horses and camels were dying and the Bani Qurayzah had betrayed them and they had also suffered immensely from wind and the rain. When Ghatafan awoke next morning and found that Quraish had gone, they too retreated. Holy Ruler deputed Hudaifa bin Al-Yaman to bring the news about the enemy. He found that the enemies were terribly frustrated and they were planning to leave the spot without achieving their objective. The Guardian of Islam sent Jabir and Abd Allah bin Umar to see that the enemy might not revert back and attack. When it was ensured that the adversaries had been badly humiliated and could not dare to turn back, Holy Ruler moved towards Medina triumphantly. History testifies that the battle of trenches was so decisive that the enemies of Islam could never muster courage to invade the Muslim state at Medina. It is quite strange that in such a big war in which nearly thirteen thousand adversaries were bent upon destroying Muslims and they confronted each other for about a month, the Ruler of Islam achieved his remarkable victory with the help of merely three thousand soldiers and losing only six Muslims compared to ten or twelve causalities of the polytheists. The war strategists are confused as to whether it was the result of the wonderful war strategy of the Ruler of Islam or the follies of the adversaries of Islam or the gift of God that the impossible task of winning a decisive battle was achieved by the Commander of Islam in an unprecedented manner. Whatever may be the case, the fact is that The Campaign of the Trench was such a war which opened the doors of Arabian Peninsula opened for the Ruler of Islam and whoever dared to face him was liquidated shamefully from the face of the earth.

NOTES

1. Dr. Ahmad A. Zidan, "The Battles of Prophet" (Islamic INC Publishers and Distributors, Egypt, 1997), p. 8.
2. Shafiur Rahman Al-Mubarakpuri, op. cit., p. 211.
3. *Ibid.*, 226.
4. Dr. Ahmad A. Zidan, op. cit., p. 67.
5. Shafiur Rahman Al-Mubarakpuri, op. cit., p. 268.
6. *Ibid.*, p. 279.
7. Dr. Ahmad A. Zidan, op. cit., p. 79.
8. Abdul Hameed Siddiqui, op. cit., p. 215.
9. *Ibid.*, pp. 220-21.

5

The Minor Battles Confronted by the Chief of Islam

It was the graciousness of the Ruler of Islam and his power of tolerance and forgiveness that he tolerated the dirty scheming, treacherous plots, dangerous revolts and unbearable nuisances of Banu Qurayza one after the other despite a treaty between them and despite reminding them of the terms of the treaty time and again. During normal days they held grudges against Muslims of Medina and at the slightest moment whenever they found Muslims in some kind of trouble, they stood against them along with the adversaries of Islam. They did not want to see Muslims on the soil of Medina and could never tolerate the emergence of Islam in nearby them. They were enjoying all kinds of privileges and had control over the economy of Medina but still they were not satisfied. The Ruler of Islam was pushed to the wall and was compelled to take some stringent and deterrent action only when he found that they had stabbed at his back. They violated the treaty and helped the invading forces of Quraish, Bedouins, Jews and other polytheists especially in such areas where their women folk were lodged for protection. Had the Ruler of Islam not acted wisely and the God's help would not have come, they would have succeeded along with the adversaries of Islam in removing Islam and the Leader of Islam from the face of the earth for all times to come.

THE INVASION OF BANU QURAYZA

Holy Ruler was terribly upset by the treachery of the Banu Qurayza. Despite their treaty with Muslims and an assurance from their sides that they would not betray Muslims, they sided with Quraish, Banu Ghatafan and others at a time when Muslims were in a very critical situation. They had collected one thousand and five hundred swords, two thousand spears, three hundred armours, five hundred shields and a large arsenal.[1] Had it not been due to the game plan of Nu'aym and the God-given help through severe cold and rain that Muslims were bound to be liquidated from the map of the world for ever. Holy Prophet decided to teach a lesson to Jews who had betrayed Muslims during their adverse phase and had treacherously sought shelter within the strong towers of their refuge. When they were surrounded by Muslims and found no way out, they started consultations. On their request Holy Commander allowed Abu Lubabah to meet the Jews and advise them accordingly. He met and heard their vows and the cries of women and children but he could not muster courage to speak in their favour despite possessing some soft corner for them. Ka'b suggested them to embrace Islam since many of them had accepted the Holy Prophet as the Messenger of Lord but they refused saying, they would prefer death over accepting Islam. A few of the young Jews secretly aligned themselves with Muslim troops and accepted Islam for they had heard that in very near future a Messenger of God would emerge among them who would conquer all of those who would oppose him. After a siege of nearly twenty-five days during which only a few arrows and javelins were thrown, they surrendered unconditionally and requested that they be tried by a member of Arab tribe of which they were the followers. Holy Ruler accepted their unreasonable condition for the captives were generally judged by the laws of the conquerors rather than the customs and traditions of the vanquished. He deputed Sa'd bin Mu'dah, a former ally. Strangely, the judge upon whose favour they were counting condemned their able bodied men to death and their women and children to slavery. The judgment was accepted by the Muslims. Only one woman of the Jews was killed for killing a Muslim fighter Khalid bin Suwaid by throwing grinding stone upon him. The rest of the women captives were sent to Najd to be exchanged for weaponry and horses. Those Jews who accepted Islam were treated most honourably. Their properties, possessions and belongings were not touched. The war booty including arms, armours, clothes, food items and possessions were collected and it was divided among the warriors after keeping a fifth for God, orphans and needy and three shares to horsemen and one to the infantry fighter. Holy Ruler married Rehana bint Amr bin Khannqah to have the good relations with the vanquished clan. The defeat of Banu Qurayza brought a tremendous solace to Muslims. Muslims were always afraid of the Jews because of their deep seated animosity for Muslims as well as their treacherous qualities. Once they were out they had no danger from within and from without.

THE ELIMINATION OF SALAM BIN ABI AL-HUQUAIQ (ABU RAFI)

Soon after the battle of Trenches and Qurayza Holy Commander made it a point to send punitive expeditions to discipline all those Jewish, Bedouin and hostile tribes of nearby Medina and the surrounding areas which were posing challenge to the Islamic State. Salam bin Abi Al-Huquaiq was a hardened criminal. He had supported the enemies of Islam at the time of Battle of Trenches with immense wealth, resources and troops. He not only used to incite the Arab and Jewish tribes against Muslims but also maligned the Ruler of Islam. One day a rival of Al-Aws sought the permission of the Prophet of Islam to kill Salam to achieve merit equal to the level of Al-Aws who had killed another Jewish criminal named Ka'b bin Al-Ashraf. The Prophet permitted them and Abdullah bin 'Ateeq with four of his colleagues marched to Khaibar where Huquaiq was protected in a strong fort. Abdullah any how managed to enter into the fort in disguise and despite several odds killed the enemy of Islam and conveyed the good news to the Prophet of Islam.

THE HUMILIATION OF BANI BAKR CLAN

Similarly, Holy Guardian sent a troop of thirty Muslims under the command of Muhammad bin Maslamah to the habitation of Bani Bakr tribe to teach them the lesson for harming Muslims. The believers attacked them and compelled them to flee leaving plenty of booty which was captured by the Muslims. The platoon of the thirty faithful also brought with them a strong disbeliever Thumamah bin Uthal Al-Hanafi, the chief of Bani Hanifa who had been dispatched by Musailmah, the Liar to assassinate Holy Prophet. He was kept tied down to a pole near the Prophet's mosque but finally forgiven by the Prophet of Islam. He embraced Islam and not only refused to pay to Makkans from Yamama, a suburb of Makkah without Prophet's permission but also remained firm on his newly acquired faith.

ATTACK UPON BANI LIHYAN

Bani Lihyan was a cunning and dangerous tribe. It had treacherously killed ten companions of Holy Prophet. Since it was located deep in the desert of Hijaj on the borders of Makkah, it was not advisable to take revenge upon them till Quraish were powerful. However, after the collapse of the combined power of the adversaries of Islam at Battle of Trenches, it was an opportune time for Muslims to rush upon the tribe and teach them lesson for their harming Muslims during their odd days. Holy Ruler marched with two hundred warriors in the year six Hijri. He adopted a technical approach in reaching Batn Gharran, where his companion were martyred and invoked Allah's mercy upon them. The news of his troops reached Bani Lihyan and they fled to mountain tops and thus remained out of his reach. When he was returning, the Steward of Islam sent ten horsemen to Kura' Al-Ghamm near Makkah with a view to instill fear amoung Quraish of his increasing influence in the area.

INVASIONS ON NEARBY HOSTILE TRIBES

There were several tribes which had been creating problems for Muslims since long. It was now an opportune time to settle the scores with them. In six Hijri, 'Ukasha bin Al-Mishan attacked Bani Asad at Al-Ghamir. The tribe fled leaving behind two hundred camels which were captured. Muhammad bin Maslamah set out with a strong force, ambushed one hundred men of Bani Tha'labah in Dhil Qassa and liquidated all of them save Muhammad bin Maslamah who escaped badly wounded. Abu 'Ubaidah bin Al-Jarrah at the head of forty men caught Bani Tha'labah at Dhil Qassa but they too fled leaving tremendous booty. Zaid bin Haritha, with the help of a woman marched along with his warriors towards Al-Jumum, the habitation of Bani Saleem in the same year and made many of them captives and got a lot of war booty. In six Hijri, Zaid bin Haritha heading one hundred and seventy horsemen looted the camels of Quraish led by Abul-'As, the son-in-law of the Prophet. Abul-'As sought refuse in the house of Zainab, his wife and on her recommendation the whole booty was voluntarily and willingly returned to Abul-'As who soon after embraced Islam and was united with his wife Zainab. In the same year Zaid commanding fifteen men raided Bani Tha'labah and captured their twenty camels but could not capture the tribe as they fled as usual. In the same year while Zaid bin Haritha with his twelve soldiers was on a reconnaissance mission at Wadi Al-Qura to observe the moments of the enemy, he was attacked and nine Muslims were killed and he along with rest of his colleagues managed to escape. In the year eight Hijri, before the Treaty of Al-Hudaibiyah, Abu 'Ubaidah bin Al-Jarrah commanding three hundred men set in the toe of the caravan of Quraish. This invasion is called Al-Khabat (diluted yoghurt) because the Muslim army felt the extreme shortage of food and they had to consume the diluted yoghurt. They were compelled to eat the meat of nine camels at three stages. It was because of sperm-whale called Al-Anbar that they were saved and returned home safely.

THE FORAY OF BANI AL-MUSTALIQ (AL MURAYSI)

The Ghazwah or the Battle of Bani Al-Mustaliq was not so important politically, strategically or militarily as it was historically significant since it had unnecessarily attracted the attention of many historians and biographers of the Holy

Prophet due to malicious propaganda created by the enemies of Islam. It caused internal dissensions among Muslims. Had Holy Prophet not handled it tactfully and resolutely it would have caused immense harm to Islam and as well as Muslim community. Another significance of this battle is its relevance with Prophet's marriage with Juwayriyya daughter of al-Harith and lastly, its connection with the sinister slander of Aisha wife of the Holy Prophet. When hypocrites like Abdullah bin Ubai realized that it was difficult to confront Muslims militarily since they were a different people not due to their material superiority, multitude of troops or equipment but due to the noble values, exemplary conduct and piety that were infused in them by the Prophet of Islam. They, therefore, decided to unleash a baseless, false and slanderous campaign against the Holy Prophet which was snubbed in the bud.

When the Holy Prophet came to know in the 6 Hijri that Bani Al-Mustaliq, a clan of Khuza'ah tribe under the leadership of Abou Dirar was mobilizing Arab tribes in the vicinity of Makkah with a view to assassinate the Holy Prophet, he deputed Buraidah bin al-Haseeb al-Aslami to verify the facts. When the Prophet became sure of the ill intentions of the enemies he immediately seized the initiative and quickly marched with his two divisions of the Emigrants and the Helpers commanded by Abu Bakr and Sa'd bin Ubadah respectively in order to dent the enemies. The Muslim army camped near a well called al-Muraysi which was not too far from enemy concentration. Having heard of Muslims' march the Arabs fled away and the arrow shooting went on for an hour and finally Muslims encircled them and the enemy was defeated. Only one Muslim, Hisham bin al-Khattab was accidentally killed by a fellow Muslim and the enemy lost ten men. Banu Mustaliq realized that it was futile to fight and hence they surrendered. They were made captives and their cattle were confiscated.

THE TRUCE OF HUDAYBIYAH

During the six years since the Prophet of Islam moved to Medina, he did not get any opportunity even in the sacred months of Ramadan and Shawwal to visit Kabah as he was involved in conflicts, battles, skirmishes and wars. In the sixth Hijri he saw a dream that he was entering the sacred sanctuary of Kabah with his head shaved in security with his companions holding its key and performing the ceremonies of Umrah (lesser pilgrimage). The Prophet of Islam told his companions to make preparations. They bought seventy camels in all to sacrifice them at Makkah at the time of the pilgrimage and give their meat to the needy. Holy Prophet mounted the camel and marched towards Kabah along with fifteen hundred Muslims including his wife Umm Salamah whose name was decided after the draw of lots. They carried no weapons except sheathed, swords and hunting equipments for they did not have any intention to quarrel with anybody. As they reached Dhi Hulaifa, he ordained that the sacrificial animals be garlanded and all Muslims donned Al-Ihram, the pilgrims dress.

Holy Prophet on his arrival at Makkah sent a man of Khuza'ah to bring back the reaction of Quraish. He was informed that the roads to Makkah were blocked and large number of slaves as well as a huge army had gathered to confront him. Prophet consulted his companions and they told him that they would not fight till they would be stopped from performing Umrah. Makkans were in dilemma since according to their own laws and customs they could not stop more than one thousand people from entering Kabah but side by side they were afraid that if they did so, the prestige of Quraish would be affected immensely and the fame of Muslims and Islam would spread throughout Arabia. To find out any solution, the Quraish also assembled and decided that they would oppose Prophet's entry to Makkah at every cost. When the pilgrims reached Usfan their scout brought the news that Quraish had sent Khalid along with two hundred horsemen to prevent their entry. Holy Prophet with the help of a man of Aslam followed a difficult and tedious route and without confronting Khalid reached the pass leading to Hudaybiyah, situated at the extremity of the sacred territory. Khalid finally realized that the Muslims had arrived and he informed the Quraish accordingly.

Holy Prophet rode on his beloved camel Qaswa and moved for pilgrimage but the moment they crossed the pass and reached a place known as Thaniyat Al-Marar, the she camel knelt down and refused to move ahead. Holy Prophet asked Qaswa to move and she quickly moved and carried him down to the edge of Hudaibiyah followed by others. Prophet asked his companions to camp there near a well with scanty water. While the Holy Prophet was camping at Hudaibiyah, Budail bin Warqa' Al Khuzai came with some celebrities of Khuzah tribe and asked him his purpose of visiting the place. Holy Prophet replied that he had come to perform the pilgrimage and not to fight but if he would be stopped, he would resist. The envoy went back and informed the Quraish accordingly. Quraish sent another person named Mikraz bin Hafs.

On seeing him Prophet said that he was cunning and a treacherous man. He was given the same answer. He was followed by Al-Hulays of the Bani al-Harith of the clans of Kinnah. When he saw the sacrificial animals standing in array, he returned without conversing with the Prophet and told them that the Prophet was a pious man and his intentions were good. When the Quraish differed with his views, he told them point blank that either they allowed him to do the pilgrimage or he would withdraw all men from their soil. They persuaded him to bear with them till they reached some definite conclusion. In the meantime, Urwah bin Masu'd Ath Thaqif had arrived at the camp and started behaving with the Prophet as equal. His objectionable postures were corrected by the companions of the Prophet with threatening gestures. He told the Quraish that "I have been to Chosroes in his kingdom and Caesar in his kingdom and the Negus in his kingdom, but never have I seen a king among a people like Muhammad among his companions. If he makes his ablutions they would not let the water thereof fall on the ground; if a hair of his falls down, they vie with each other in order to secure that. They will not abandon him for anything in any case. Do what you please."[2] Some of the mischievous persons from among Quraish tried to create problems but they were caught and let go. After getting the feedback from various envoys Quraish finally became soft. However, since nothing was materialized, Holy Prophet decided to send one of his envoys to Makkans. On the advice of Umar it was decided that Uthman be sent there because of his following and influence. Uthman went there and met all the chiefs of Quraish and convinced them that they had come to perform the pilgrimage. However, if they were stopped, sever resistance would come from their side. When Uthman did not come, Muslims began to feel some foul play from the side of Quraish. It was at that time that Muslims took a solemn pledge at the hand of the Prophet that they would sacrifice their lives to avenge the death of their companion and stand firmly by their Prophet under all circumstances. This pledge is known as "Bay'at Ar-Ridwan". When Quraish came to the conclusion that Muslims were bent upon performing Umrah and nobody would be able to stop them, they thought it better to enter into a treaty in March, 628 which is known by the name of "The Truce of Al-Hudaibiyah".

Quraish sent Suhayl along with two clansmen namely Mikraz and Huwaytib to conclude the treaty. Some disputes arose with regard to the Preamble which were amicably settled by the Holy Prophet giving ample concessions and latitude to Quraish. When Ali started the letter with Bi-ism-Allah ar-Rahman ar-Rahim that is, "In the name of Allah, the Most Beneficent, the Most Merciful", Suhayl bin 'Amr said he knew nothing about al-Rahman. He asked him to write Bi-ismka Allahumma, that is "In the name of God". Muslims felt annoyed and some of them cried and said that they would write nothing save what they want but Holy Prophet over ruled them. When Ali wrote, "This is what Muhammad, the Messenger of Allah has agreed to with." Suhayl bin "Amr replied that if they had accepted him as the Messenger of God, the wars would not have been fought. He, therefore, said that "Write Muhammad the son of Abdullah". Ali had already written "the Messenger of God" and thus declined to make any change in it by his own hand. Holy Prophet asked him to cross those words out but when he found Ali reluctant, he himself crossed them out. Muslims considered these changes as the symptoms of weakness and thus resisted but kept mum due to the agreeing of Holy Prophet. The text continued as follows:

> They have consented to stop war activities for ten years, during which time both parties will live in full security and not commit any violence upon each other, on condition that whoever comes to Muhammad of Quraish without the leave of his guardian, Muhammad shall return him to them; but whoever comes to Quraish of those who are with Muhammad, they shall not be returned. There shall be no subterfuge and no treachery. And whoever desires to join Muhammad or enter into treaty with him should have the liberty to do so; and whoever wishes to enter the bond and pact of Quraish may do so. Muhammad shall depart from us this present year and the next year, we shall go out from Makkah and he shall enter it with his companions but they shall not stay in Makkah for more than three days. They shall not come back armed but can bring with them swords only sheathed in scabbards and these shall be kept in bags.[3]

It was during the period when the treaty was not signed that Abu Jandal, the son of suhayl came chained and fatigued and wanted to be saved from the clutches of the polytheists. Muslims persuaded Holy Prophet to provide him protection but the Prophet of Islam despite having soft corner for Abu Jandal returned him to Quraish as per the terms of the treaty. Muslims condition was very pathetic. They were considering themselves cheated and defeated but kept quiet because of Holy Prophet since they knew that apparently they were losers but may be that there was Lord's greatest blessing in it in the disguised form. When the treaty was concluded Prophet slaughtered the animals which he had brought with him, shaved his head and moved towards Medina. The future events showed that the treaty of Hudaibiyah was not a humiliation for Muslims but it was indeed a victory for them. They got enough time to relax and propagate their religion due to the peace brought about by the execution of the treaty. As a matter of fact within a short period of time not only the grace and dignity of Islam spread far and wide but people joined Islam in multitude and Makkah was conquered in no time and the Quraish were subdued for all times to come.

THE BATTLE OF KHAIBAR

After the truce was made with Makkah, the Ruler of Islam diverted his attention to North of Medina where the Jews and the Najd tribes were posing a constant threat to the capital of Islamic State and debarring Muslims from spreading the message of Islam in the world. There was a concentration of Jewish power in Khaibar 80-90 miles north of Medina. Khaibar was always a hotbed of politics, intrigues and conspiracies. Whenever Muslims were in trouble, the Jews of Khaibar exploited the situation and provoked the enemies of Islam against them because they were basically against Islam. The Jews of Khaibar had entered into an alliance with Banu Qurayza, Ghatafan, Quraish, Bedouins and other hostile tribes and had planned even to assassinate Holy Prophet. Khaibar was practically impregnable. It was a strongly fortified territory guarded by a group of fortresses among which the fort of Al-Kamas was located on an inaccessible height. Besides, the Jews of Khaibar had ten thousand warriors and they had received the assurance of four thousand soldiers from Ghatafan. Moreover, the exiled Bani-Nadir and the Qurayza tribes were there which could go to any extent to defeat Muslims.

Despite these challenges, Holy Ruler did not abandon his campaign. He marched with his fourteen hundred fighters towards Khaibar. First of all he adopted the route along Isra Mountain and halted in a valley called Ar-Raji which fell between Khaibar and Ghatafan in order to block the entry of four thousand soldiers of Ghatafan who were to reach Khaibar for the help of the Jews. He adopted the strategy of winning the minor and less fortified forts of Jews one after the other. In the beginning he attacked the fort of Na'im where the commander of the Jews named Marhab fought bravely along with his force but he was killed by Ali. Later on his other warriors came for combat operations but they too were liquidated. Finally the fighting broke and it lasted for few days. When Jews could not face the might of Muslims, they retreated to the fortress of As-Sa'b. Muslims laid the siege of the fort for three days and this fort too was captured along with war booty and a large provision of food which was necessary for Muslims since they were practically starving due to the lack of food. Having seen Muslims moving ahead, Jews evacuated An-Natat and took shelter in the well fortified Az-Zubair which was inaccessible both for infantry and cavalry. Muslims laid the siege of the fort for three days but could not dent its formidable defensive position. It was on leaking the secret by a Jewish spy caught by Muslims about the subterranean water source that Muslims could block the water supply and undermined the strength of the enemy. Compelled by circumstances the Jews came out and fought fiercely killing some Muslims and losing ten Jews but they lost the fort to Muslims. The Jews moved to Abi Castle and fortified them within the confines of the fort but there too Muslim cornered them and entered into the fort and compelled them to flee to the fort of An-Nizar which in their opinion was a powerful fort and too immune to be stormed by Muslim forces. Jews threw arrows and the stones upon Muslims from the fort. Realizing the impregnability of the fort Holy Commander ordered his troops to use the innovative technique which created the cracks in the ramparts providing easy entry to Muslims. Jews ran away hither and thither leaving women and children.

Having achieved the victory over enemy forces, Holy Ruler moved towards Al-Katiba and laid the siege for fifteen days. When he was to use the rams, Jews got frightened and requested for a negotiable peace treaty. The Prophet of Islam agreed to spare their lives on the condition that they shall evacuate Khaibar and the adjacent land and also leave all gold, silver and other treasure which was in their possession. However, if they concealed anything, they would not be spared.[4] Jews handed over Al-Katiba, Al-Qamus and Al-Waqidi forts to Muslims and Khaiber came under the control of Muslims with large booty and captives. Safyah, daughter of Huyai, the chief of Bani Qurayza and Bani Nadir was taken as captive. She embraced Islam and was married to Holy Guardian of Islam at Aadd As-Sahba on the route of Madinah. The wedding of the Ruler of Islam to Safyah, the princess of the Chief after conquering one of the richest territories and obtaining large war booty was celebrated on dates and fat.

Some of the Jews who concealed the treasure and broke the conditions of the treaty were punished. As per condition of the treaty, the Jews were bound to leave Khaiber but when they approached the Prophet of Islam with the request that they be allowed to cultivate their lands in lieu of half of the produce to Muslims, he agreed. Holy Prophet divided the land of Khaiber into two parts. One part was reserved for food to be used under calamities and emergencies as well as to meet the requirement of international guests who very often visited Madinah and the other half was meant for Muslims who were present at Al-Hudaibiyah whether they were there or not. The booty was divided between 1200 footmen and 200 horsemen in the ratio of 3 shares to horsemen and one to the footman. The war booty of Khaiber not only changed the financial conditions of Muslims but it also provided great benefits to the Islamic State. After the conquest of Khaiber a Jewish women tried to poison the Prophet but he forgave her. It is quite revealing that Holy Prophet followed such a nice strategy that in the entire Khaiber operation only 16 to 18 Muslims and 93 Jews lost their lives. The rest of Khaiber also fell without shedding much blood. The people of Fadaq, a village situated to the north of Khaiber surrendered before the Prophet. However, the people of a Jewish colony named Wadi Al-Qura resisted but ultimately surrendered after losing their eleven men. Prophet of Islam concluded a treaty with them and distributed the large booty among his soldiers. The Jews of Taima were sensible. They did not resist and entered into a treaty to the effect that they receive protection in lieu of tribute paid by them. When Holy Prophet reached Medina he found that Aban bin Sa'id who had headed a unit of warriors in the absence of the Commander of Islam had already succeeded in deterring and forestalling any attempt by the sundry tribes living nearby to destabilize Medina.

THE CAMPAIGN OF MU'TAH

After returning from Hudaibiyah, Holy Prophet sent fifteen men to Dhat al Talh on the border of Syria to invite people to

Islam but all of them were brutally killed. Likewise, he had sent Al-Harith bin 'Umair Al-Azdi with a letter to the ruler of Busra but on his way back he was caught by Al-Ghassani, the governor of Al-Balqa and a close ally of Caesar, the emperor of Byzantine who beheaded him mercilessly. These events perturbed Holy Ruler since they indicated at the future confrontation of Muslims with the biggest empires of those times. Since killing the messengers and the envoys was amounted to declaring war, the Commander of Islam mobilized a mighty force of three thousand warriors under the command of Zayd bin Haritha and sent them in 629 A.D. to Mu'tah, a village on the border of Syria to teach a lesson to the adversaries of Islam. Holy Steward knew that this battle was to prove as one of the fieriest and significant battles as it was to open opportunities for Muslims for the future conquests of Christian's chiefdoms. He, therefore, gave the instructions that in the event of the martyrdom of Zayd, Ja'far bin Abu Talib should replace him and in the event of Ja'far's demise Abd Allah bin Rawahah would take his place. He ordered them not to fight but invite them towards Islam.

However, if they retaliated, they were permitted to confront them but with the proviso that they were allowed to fight merely in the cause of Islam neither breaching the covenant nor entertaining treachery. They were further warned that under no circumstance a new born, a woman, an aging man or a hermit was to be killed. Besides, neither the trees were to be cut down nor the homes of the adversaries were to be demolished. When Muslim army reached M'an, they came to know that Arabs had aligned with Byzantines and Heraclius had mobilized a hundred thousand troops and another batch consisting of hundred thousand warriors supported by Laham, Judham and Balqain was at his disposal. Muslims did not bother about the strength of the enemy but fought in the name of Allah to achieve their one of the two objectives: martyrdom or victory. They tactfully, bravely and intelligently fought losing their commanders Zayd bin Haritha, Ja'far bin Abi Talib and Abdullah bin Rawaha in succession. Finally, Khalid bin Al-Waleed took the command and fighting strategically and logistically repulsed the enemy at a safe distance and retreated his troops safely to Medina creating tremendous fear in the ranks of army, causing heavy casualties but losing merely his twelve warriors. The campaign of Muslims at Mu'tah was apparently unsuccessful since they could not take the revenge of the murder of Al-Harith. Besides, the set back to Muslims at Mu'tah encouraged the northern Arabs to mobilize a strong force to attack Medina. When the information reached Holy Commander that the tribes of Bali and Qudah'ah were collecting a larger troop on the Syrian border without the help of Byzantine empire, he sent 'Amr bin al As with three hundred fighters assisted by a cavalry of thirty men. When 'Amr realized that the enemy was in larger number he requested for additional force. Holy Prophet sent Abu Ubaydah with two hundred men. 'Amr being from the tribe of Bali was directed to take the help of Bali, Balqain and 'Udhra. As 'Amr advanced towards the habitation of Quda'a and penetrated deep in their lands with his five hundred soldiers, the enemy fled. Similarly, Holy Prophet sent Abu Qatadah with fifteen men to suppress Bani Ghatafan which was bent upon creating the problem but he defeated them badly. Some of the enemy soldiers were killed, many were captured and their properties and possessions were confiscated. Despite the setback at Mut'ah, Muslims were gainer in the sense that they certainly left the impression upon the non-believers that Muslims were indeed an entirely different people as the three thousand fighters did not hesitate to confront the mighty Byzantine force of two hundred thousand on the battle field. Their strong faith in Allah and the spiritual, moral and Godly power of the Holy Prophet brought about a tremendous change in the mindsets of the people and the tribes like Ghatafan, Fazarah, Banu Saleem Ashja, Dhubyan and so many others which were hostile to Muslims and Islam willingly accepted Islam. The campaign of Mu'tah was also important from the point of view of future adventures of Muslims outside Arabia. It actually opened the gates for Muslims for the conquest of Byzantine empire and other kingdoms of remote areas.

CONQUEST OF MAKKAH

When the Treaty of Hudaibiyah was signed, the tribes of Arabs were given the liberty to join either of the parties with which they wished to enter into alliance. As a consequence of which Banu Bakr joined Quraish and Khuza'ah joined the Prophet. They had the past enmities which subsided for a time being but ultimately they came to the forefront and Banu Bakr out of revenge attacked Khuz'ah without caring for the treaty. In their venture Quraish helped them by supplying them arms as well as manpower. When Khuza'ah people sought protection in the sacred sanctuary of Kabah, they were not spared. Nawfal, the chief of Banu Bakr chased them in the sanctuary where shedding of the blood is strictly prohibited and liquidated his adversaries. Thereupon Khuza'ah approached Holy Prophet and sought his help as per the terms of the treaty. He agreed and asked the Quraish to follow any of the following three conditions:

1. To pay blood money to the victims of Khuza'ah,
2. To break their bond with Banu Bakr, or
3. To nullify the treaty of Hudaibiyah.

The Quraish did not appreciate the gravity of situation and out of vanity said that neither they would pay blood money nor break the treaty with Banu Bakr but were prepared to declare the treaty as null and void.[5] Holy Ruler was left with no option but to face Quraish on the battle field. Abu Sufyan realized that the Quraish had committed blunder by nullifying the treaty. He went to Medina to extend the terms of treaty from two years to ten years. He met his daughter Umm Habibah, the wife of Holy Prophet, Holy Prophet himself, Abu Bakr, Umar, Ali bin Abi Talib and Fatima but all in vain. He came to Makkah and narrated all that had happened at Medina. The Quraish did not imagine that there could be a war on this issue. The Ruler of Islam made up his mind to teach a final lesson to the hot-headed Makkans. Strategically he started making preparations for war which gave the impression to the people that he was moving to face hostile tribes in Syria and the surrounding areas. As a tactical move he sent an eight-man platoon under the command of Qatada bin Rabi'i in the direction of Edam not too far from Medina. He sent the message to all Muslims of the Peninsula to mobilize immediately and be present in Medina. All Bedouins without any exception heeded to his call. Muslim army consisted of seven hundred Emigrants, four thousand Helpers with five hundred horsemen, three hundred horsemen and Bani Sulaym with a troop of cavalry of nine hundred strong joined at Qudayd and many of them joined in the way making a total of ten thousand men. After making full preparations he marched towards Makkah along with ten thousand soldiers in 8th Hijri. People were not sure of the destination of the troop. The people of Ta'if were expecting an attack upon them and many other tribes too were afraid of the imminent danger. Quraish, however, were apprehensive due to violating the conditions of the treaty but were not sure that they were going to face the music. Holy Ruler never wanted to confront the Quraish by surprise. In order to let them know about his presence as well as strength he asked the troop to disperse in all direction and lit the fire after the dark. When the Quraish saw innumerable fires burning from outside the sacred territory they were baffled and the news soon spread in Makkah that the army of the Ruler of Islam was much more than what they had expected. They hurriedly called a consultative meeting in which it was decided to send Abu Sufyan along with Hakim, Khadijah's nephew, and Budayl of Khuza'ah to mend the rapture of the pact. After meeting the Prophet they were so impressed that they came within the fold of Islam and thought it better to surrender rather than confront the Holy Prophet. In January, 630 (20 Ramadan, AH 8) Makkans surrendered before the Ruler of Islam without fighting. It was mostly because of the intercession of 'Abbas, the uncle of the Holy Prophet and the sincere efforts of Abu Sufyan that the hurdles were cleared for peaceful settlement. Victors are generally proud and arrogant and they are happy to take revenge from their victims but the Ruler of Islam proved to be an extreme type of exception which the humanity had never seen before. Holy Prophet communicated to the Makkans through Abu Sufyan that "Whoever enters the house of Abu Sufyan is safe, and whoever locks himself inside his doors is safe, and whoever enters the Mosque is safe."

Holy Ruler calmly, patiently and intelligently drew the plan for the entry of his troops within the bounds of Makkah. He had only one consideration in mind and that was to avoid bloodshed and violence as far as possible. He had decided to honour the Makkans rather than humiliating them. He made Khalid bin Al-Waleed commander to lead. Sulaim, Ghifar, Muzainah, Aslam and Juhainah tribes to enter Makkah through its lower avenues. Az-Zubair bin 'Awwam was directed to lead the left flank and enter Makkah from the upper portion and Abu 'Ubaidah took the command of the infantry and was to enter the town from the side of valley. They were given full powers but with the proviso that they would kill only those in self-defence who confronted them and subdue those who were bent upon creating chaos and confusion. There was no resistance from Makkans save from some reckless criminals led by 'Ikeimah bin Abi Jahl. Khalid triumphantly entered killing twelve of the ruffians and sacrificing two martyrs. Az-Zubair and Abu 'Ubaidah too reached their destinations and planted the flags of victory. When the people of Makkah heard of general amnesty provided to them by Holy Prophet they became happy. As a matter of fact the people of Makkah were divided. Majority was in favour of accepting Islam as they had seen the beauty of Islam and the futility of their artificial Gods. Moreover, they were highly impressed by those Arabs who had embraced Islam because there was a miraculous change in their conducts, characters and behaviour pattern. Those who were against Islam were mainly the chiefs and rich and famous men who were enjoying prosperous life due to the ignorance of their fellow men.

It was in the spirit of clemency, brotherhood, compassion and mercy that the Holy Ruler entered Makkah. He did not butcher those who had killed his beloved uncle Hamza, did not take revenge from those who had chewed Hamza's liver and mutilated his body and did not destroy those who had killed his dearest daughter. He forgave those who had tortured him, humiliated him and were after his life and pardoned those who had treated the members of his family with naked cruelty, driven them out of their dwellings and locked them in solitary confinement. He showed mercy even upon those who had inflicted awful injuries and extreme type of humiliation upon innocent men and women as well upon those who were dead.

The rebellious Makkans were at his feet and if he liked he could teach them such a lesson which their posterity remembered for all times to come.

Being a blessing upon whole mankind, he behaved mercifully forgiving all his adversaries unconditionally. It is worth noting that there were nine hardened criminals who according to all cannons of international justice should have been killed but Holy Prophet allowed the killing of only four who were the rarest of the rare. 'Ikrimah bin Abu Jahal who had attacked the forces of Khalid at the time of the entry into Makkah was pardoned, Washi, the murderer of Hamzah, the uncle of the Prophet was forgiven, Hind who chewed the lever of Hamza was given amnesty and Habar who had attacked Prophet's daughter with spear too was granted mercy. Likewise, he took no action against Fudalah bin Umair who had attempted on his life and exempted Safwan bin Omaiyah, the chief of Quraish who was the root cause of many evils. He entered Kabah with pure heart, clean conscience and full of pity and mercy. He purified the sanctuary by removing the 360 idols and thanked Lord for fulfilling his mission. He declared the holy status of Kabah till the Day of Judgment and prohibited shedding of blood within its limits. He also stopped uprooting its shrubs, cutting trees or to chase its game or to pick up a fallen thing. He assigned the duty of door-keeping of Al-Kabah and supplying water to the pilgrims as well as the key of Al-Kabah to Uthman bin Talhah and his descendants forever. When the time of prayer came Bilal ascended Al-Kabah and called for prayer. On that very day Holy Prophet entered the house of 'Umm Hani, washed and offered his prayers of victory. The victory of Makkah was a decisive victory for Holy Prophet. It crushed polytheism and paganism and raised the banner of Islam. Makkans embraced Islam willingly and those Arabian tribes that were watching the outcome of this campaign also appreciated the Holy Prophet and the multitude among them came voluntarily within the fold of Islam.

THE BATTLE OF HUNAIN

After the conquest of Makkah many tribes of Arab had surrendered before the Ruler of Islam realizing the fact that it was futile to confront the emerging power of Islam. However, there were some furious, famous and proud tribes like Bani Hilal, Nasr, Jasham, Sa'd bin Bakr Thaqif and Hawazin who were not willing to yield before the Holy Prophet. They knew that they were strong enough to face the might of Islam and hence they met Malik bin 'Awf An-Nasri and decided to attack Muslim forces. Malik bin Awf directed all his people to carry with them their camels, cattle, wealth, women, children and treasure with them to Awtas which was the valley near Hawazen and not too far from Hunain so that they may not flee seeing the enemy strength but fight bravely to protect them. Many sensible people including Durand bin As-Simmah tried to stop him from doing this but he remained firm.

When the Holy Prophet came to know of enemy intentions through his secret agents, he marched towards Hunain with his twelve thousand strong fighters which included 2000 warriors from Makkans. The tribes of Hawazin and Thaqif along with their allies equipped with their four thousand sharp shooters and warriors had already reached Hunain and taken strategic positions. Muslims were a bit complacent due to the strength of their armed forces. As soon as Khalid accompanied by the fighters of Banu Sulyam entered the narrow, steep and difficult pass, suddenly he faced the shower of arrows from all sides. His entry was blocked and Muslims were confused and confounded. Many of them especially the newly convert Makkans fled hither and thither. Holy Prophet was left almost unguarded with few of his companions and relatives on a hillock. Seeing the miserable condition of the force, he called the troop to come back and fight. As soon as the Muslim warriors heard the call of the Prophet, they reassembled and fought bravely as a consequence of which many enemy soldiers were killed including seventy men of Thaqif. Some of the adversaries fled to Ta'if, a few to Nakklah and others to Awtas. Muslims followed them and killed a few of their important dignitaries. However, many of them took shelter in the strong and well protected fort of Ta'if leaving twenty-four thousand camels, forty thousand sheep, four thousand ounces of silver and six thousand captives. Holy Prophet ordered to confine the war booty at Al-J'irah under the command of Mas'ud bin 'Amr Al-Ghifari.

THE CAMPAIGN OF TA'IF

The campaign of Ta'if was basically the part and parcel of the invasion of Hunain because after their defeat at Hunain most of the defeated troops of Hawazin and Thaqif along with their commander Malik bin 'Awf An-Nasri had sought shelter in the fort of Ta'if. Therefore, after accomplishing his task at Hunain and confining the war booty at Al-Ji'ranah, the Ruler of Islam sent Khalid to Al-Ta'if commanded by one thousand warriors. He himself moved towards the enemy concentration passing through Nakhlah Al-Yamaniyah, and Qam Al-Manazil destroying the fort of Malik bin 'Awf at Laiyah. Finally, he reached Ta'if and camped near the fort and ordered his troops to siege the fort along with their inhabitants. Enemy resorted to arrow-shooting and rock-hurling which killed twelve Muslims and injured many. Thereafter, Holy Prophet took position at a higher location and shelled the castle which created many gaps through which Muslim warriors tried to enter the fort but failed due to pouring down molten hot iron upon them. A call was given to the inhabitants of the fort that he who would come out would be set free. Only twenty-three people came out and they were set free and arrangement was made for their upkeep. To force the enemy to surrender, Holy Ruler asked his troops to destroy some of their valuable Assets. When the Muslims caused some damage, the enemy begged the mercy of the Ruler of Islam and the process was discontinued with immediate effect. Holy Prophet lifted the siege and moved towards Al'Ji'ranah. Before distributing the war booty, Holy Prophet waited for about ten days in the hope that Hawazin tribe might come and reclaim their possessions after declaring their repentance. When they did not come, the booty was divided between the Quraish and the Helpers in such a way that greater portion went to the chiefs and celebrities of Makkah and lesser to the Helpers which created some heart-burning among the helpers but upon the intervention of Holy Prophet they were completely satisfied. As soon as the booty was distributed, various delegations representing several tribes came which included his foster uncle, foster mothers and sisters. He was moved by their emotions and returned all that which came to him and his members of family as their shares. He appealed to others to surrender their shares voluntarily and all of them gave back their captive women and children. He also provided a garment as a gift to every captive.

THE MARCH TO TABUK

The defeat of Persians at the hands of Romans had provided some solace to Muslims because the Persians had withdrawn their forces from Syria and Egypt. Muslims were, however, always apprehensive from the side of Heraclius, the emperor of Byzantines, though heart to heart he never wanted to confront the Muslims due to the dream that he had seen. Information reached Medina that Heraclius had provided one year's salary to his troops for fighting Muslims and he had aligned with the tribes of Lakhim, Ghassan, Amilah and Judham and their forces had reached as far as Balqa. Holy Ruler declared his intention to march to Syria. He ordered the people of Makah and allied tribes to send their armed forces to Madinah for onward movement to Syria. The year 630 was a drought year and the early October was a hot month and the shortage of water had made the situation more repressive. Moreover, it was a season when the fruits and the crops had ripened and many people were not willing to participate in the venture. Over and above this, Muslims were short of funds and they did not have enough resources to buy weapons, camels, horses and equipment for a journey which was tedious and was to pass through scorching desert. Muslims contributed lavishly at the call of Holy Prophet and a huge army with thirty thousand warriors and ten thousand horses was assembled. Hypocrites stayed behind after submitting their excuse and those who had no money too were permitted to leave behind. The army moved only after sun set because in the day time there was no shade except the shadows of the barren rocks which were too hot to provide any comfort and the soil of the desert was burning as the hot coal. The dusk could bring some relief to men and animals but the nights were short. The nomads, the Bedouins, the young and old felt the fatigue but

Holy Prophet never faltered despite the fact that he had several responsibilities to perform and he was neither a Nomad nor Bedouin nor young. Finally, the entire force of Muslims reached Tabuk on the frontiers of Roman Empire. It was a cool, green, spacious and shady place. When he reached the destination he found that the borders were completely calm.

Those who propagate false information among the people that the Ruler of Islam spread his kingdom by mere power of force should know that he had reached Syria with his thirty thousand forces and there was no power on earth to stop him from bringing Damascus and parts of Syria under his domination. Holy Ruler did not fight. He was fully satisfied because his objective had already been achieved. He had succeeded in showing to the Arabs and the surrounding people that the Empire of Islam had become a reality. It was a force to reckon with for the Ruler of Islam was an exceptional person. When he could reach Tabuk with thirty thousand fighters without caring for the scorching heat and unsurmounting obstacles merely on rumours, he could dare to face his enemy anywhere in the plains, mountains, oceans, plateaus and deserts.

THE PURPOSE OF SHOWING THE WAR BATTLES FOUGHT BY THE RULER OF ISLAM

The purpose of writing about the wars fought by the Guide of Islam was to convince the people that the wars that he fought were such which were never fought by any individual or a group any time on any part of the world since time immemorial. Conventional wars were fought generally by Emperors, Kings, Monarchs, Chiefs, Warriors, Dictators and Savages to win territories and subjugate people, loot properties and possessions, capture women and children, impose their ideologies and belief systems, plunder orchards and farm lands and take revenge and to teach lessons to the adversaries. Besides, these wars were confined to the worldly benefits and name and fame only. They had nothing to do with the guidance of the people, their betterments and their contentment and their salvation. No king fought any war to bring people from ignorance to sanity, no emperor launched any campaign to remove the evils of the society and to make people civilized and enlightened, no monarch attacked any country to make their material, worldly and after-life meaningful and purposeful and no chief ever mounted the mighty aggression upon any country with a view to give the code of conduct, ways of living and leading them on the path of piety, progress, harmony and peaceful co-existence. Moreover, the wars fought in the past mostly pertained to the confrontation or engagement between two or more adversaries burning with hatred and ill-will. They benefitted the conquerors and a certain segment of the society at the cost of others. Over and above this, they were bloody and violent in nature and were fought just to win the war by hook or crook without following any code of conduct or principles. As against this, the wars which the Guide of Islam fought had nothing to do with any of the objectives mentioned above.

First of all he fought no war from his side because he never wanted anything from anybody. On the other hand, he wanted to give everything to others and for this purpose he needed no wars. It is very interesting to note that for thirty years people called him most trustworthy and most truthful but they raised their swords against him when he said that "Believe only in One True God instead of several false gods and be good to others and lead a pious, sin and crime-free and purposeful life." What was wrong in it? Were the Quraish and others justified in launching bloody wars against the Prophet of Islam for inviting them towards a righteous path? Despite their follies and persecutions he remained steadfast and never raised arms even against his self-defence. He avoided conflicts till the last stage and when he realized that his enemies were bent upon removing him from the scene, he migrated to Medina to save bloodshed. It was not he but his adversaries that did not leave him alone even at the distance 210 miles but attacked upon him, he tried to pacify the aggressors with a view to avoid bloody conflict. He fought all the wars imposed upon him for the benefit of entire mankind merely to bring them from darkness to light and to make their worldly life comfortable and peaceful and to provide them solace and salvation in the hereafter without any difference of caste, creed, colour, place of birth and belief systems. The Prophet of Islam never considered any segment his opponent or enemy and therefore, there was no question of fighting war with any adversary. He treated all human beings as his brothers and sisters for he believed that all were created by the same Lord and all were the children of Adam and Eve. He simply wanted to bring his own people on the right path since he was convinced that they had deviated from their right path due to ignorance, vanities and personal considerations. Thus, the wars and battles that the Ruler of Islam fought against his adversaries would surely and certainly convince the readers without any shred of doubt that they were not his creations.

It is the considered opinion of all the war experts that wars are always fought with vengeance but if one looks at the wars fought by Holy Ruler one would find that there was not a slightest tinge of vengeance in any war. Historians are witness to the fact that no woman was raped, no widow or the divorcee was molested, no child was abused, no orphan was harmed, no aged or handicapped was troubled, no clergy or religious authority was humiliated, no eminent man of the society was brought to knees and no citizen who did not raise arms was tortured. Likewise, no house was looted, no farm was destroyed, no meadow was ruined, no plantation was destroyed, no church was touched, no monastery was harmed and no synagogue was burnt. One does not find the victorious Islamic cavalry crushing people, conquering soldiers snatching valuables from people and the commanders of Islamic units thundering in egos and vanities. Instead, one would find them in the cities with humiliation and humbleness. They treated the vanquished with love and compassion, protected the sanctity of their Holy books and religious places and provided adequate safety and security to their lives, honours, dignities, possessions and properties. What to talk of taking revenge from the opponents, the Commander of Islam did not take any revenge against those who killed his daughter, tore apart limbs of his uncle and humiliated his kith and kin.

It is also the fact of history that when he was pushed to the wall and was compelled to fight, he showed his miracles and inherent qualities. The mightiest commanders of his time bent down, the furious fighters ran way, the dauntless soldiers bowed down and the renowned warriors surrendered before him. He fought courageously and bravely and broke all their defensive lines, tore apart the strongest walls of their forts and fortresses, shattered their strengths and might and broke down their backbones. He was indeed a wonderful general, extremely alert commander, most insightful marshal, highly righteous military leader, immensely farsighted chieftain and exceptionally immaculate steward. The approach he adopted in the initial stages to avoid war, the tools that he used to convince the people to follow his sanity call, the technique he followed in planning his strategies, the way he used logistic support, the mode in which he made triumphant maneuvers and the manner in which he fought the wars following humanistic principles and the procedure which he adopted while dealing with war criminals and the vanquished would certainly give the impression to everybody that the Commander of Islam was indeed a greatest military leader of all times.

The war strategist generally say that everything is fair in love and war but the Guide of Islam never resorted to treachery, deceit and stabbing at the back. He always fought the wars according to the glorious principles of war and ordered his warriors every time not to start the wars from their sides unless they were attacked by enemy forces. He was extremely kind to living beings. What to talk of killing innocent and helpless people, he cared for the lives of birds and animals. He repeatedly emphasized that the life of a small bird was extremely precious and could not be taken without sufficient reasons. Whoever kills the swallow or even a more insignificant bird than that shall be answerable to the Lord.[6] He warned people not be harsh and unkind to birds and animals. He never attacked enemy forces in the dark of the night but fought only after the day break when the enemy was prepared to face him on the battle field. He strictly warned his people not to kill a wounded person nor to run after a fleeing one or kill a captive. He forbade his soldiers to kill an infant child and deform the corpse of a dead soldier and raise their swords upon weaklings and those who were armless.

He never allowed his men to kill any envoy or one who came to enter into any covenant. He ruled that the killing of non-combatants that is those who did not take any part in the war such as women and children, the aged and the infirm, the blind, the imbecile, the travelers, and the man devoted to monastic services was forbidden in Islam.[7] He told the soldiers not to kill the old and verging on death, nor children and babies nor females. He also warned them not to steal anything from war booty and not to collect all those things which fell to them outside the battlefields. He directed his commanders not to lay hands on any women or slave, not to burn the enemy and not to slay any living being without sufficient reason even if it was hen. He strictly forbade wanton destruction of enemy's crop and property at the time of invasion and after the conquest. He forbade his soldiers to make loud noise on the battle field save glorifying the grace of the God. It is interesting to note that after the demise of the Ruler of Islam, the four caliphs who succeeded him strictly followed the rules of the war as laid down by their Leader. The first caliph Abu Bakr told his soldiers while bidding them farewell to the campaign of Syria that "Do not commit treachery, nor depart from the right path. Do not mutilate, nor kill a child, nor aged man, nor a woman. Do not destroy a palm tree, nor harm it with fire and do not cut any fruit tree. You must not slay any of the flocks or herds of camels, save for your subsistence. You are likely to pass by people who have devoted their lives to monastic services; leave them to what they have devoted their lives. You are likely to find, likewise, people who will present to you meals of many kinds. You may eat but do not forget to mention the name of Allah."[8]

It was the practice in those days to kill all the male members of the rulers including infant children and bring their women under their harem as well as to enslave and kill and torture those who were captives. This was done because it was believed those days that such persons were the potential enemies. It was, however, a strange coincidence that those who came under the purview of the Guide of Islam did not turn out to be his potential enemies but loved him more than their lives, honour, possessions and dearest and nearest. Thanks to the

Steward of Islam that he behaved nicely with the defeated rulers and neither killed their male members nor destroyed their palaces and dwellings nor brought their wives under his harem. It was because of his compassionate attitude towards his enemies that minimum casualties were committed in the battles he fought during his life time. It is quite pleasant to note that in all the eighty-two encounters which took place between Muslims and non-Muslims during the days of the Ruler only one thousand and eighteen people lost their lives on both sides. "Out of this two hundred and fifty-nine were Muslims and the remaining seven hundred and fifty-nine belonged to opposite camp."[9] If we compare the causalities in wars we find that in World War I ten million soldiers were killed and equal number of civilians lost their lives and twenty million died on account of epidemics and famines throughout the world as an aftermath of war. Likewise, in the Second World War twenty-two million people were killed and thirty-four million were wounded. Similarly, in Korean War more than one million military persons and four million civilians were killed. In the same way, the religious wars that Charles the Great fought 4500 pagan Saxons were cold bloodedly killed. History is witness to the fact that in the invasions by Europeans many million people were killed in North America, South America, Africa and Asia. So also several millions were killed when Abraham Lincoln fought the war to free the slaves, Lenin established his communist rule in Soviet Union and Mao Tse-tung followed his reformatory movements.

His main mission was to guide people on the path of truth, justice and righteousness. He wanted to spread the message of Islam among people peacefully without any coercion but his adversaries did not allow him to do so. He did not use the sword to spread Islam but his adversaries raised their swords to stop him from conveying the peaceful message of Islam. They killed his envoys, stopped his companions from preaching Islam by force and when they did not succeed, they planned his assassination. He persistently requested them to allow him and his companions to convey the message of God to all people irrespective of their caste, creed, colour, sex, place of birth and belief systems but they stood against him and challenged him to confront them. Being the best master and the greatest hero of all times, he did not hesitate to confront them and without any exception he defeated all of them on all battle fields. The way he mobilized the battalions from scratch, the manner in which he raised their morale despite lack of equipments, the mode in which he trained the warriors, the style in which he imbibed in them the spirit of do and die speak volumes of his military expertise never seen before in the world. None of the battle that he fought was lost as a consequence of his hasty planning, lack of foresight, defective logistic support, shortage of manpower or wrong implementation. Likewise, he was never found lacking in selecting strategic locations, placing his troops in most advantageous positions and providing them safe passage under extremely odd situations. He never committed any technical error in army mobilization and always led his troops from front and caused fear, confusion and chaos among enemy forces. He was never caught unaware, napping or unprepared but preempted all the enemy moves by his excellent skill, exceptional wisdom and exemplary alertness. The temporary setback in any of the battles was not caused by his misjudgment about mobilizing the forces in the wrong strategic positions or in selecting incapable commanders or due to the defective choice of the soldiers or because of placing them in unfavourable situations. In Uhud worldly charms and in Hunain the weak faith of the new converts caused some temporary setbacks to Muslims but thanks to the genius of the Commander of Islam that he stood fast alone facing the whole enemy might and by his guts and intuition he not only thwarted the adversary's aims but also turned the apparent defeat into a manifest victory. When he was involved in series of battles, he did not forget his basic purpose of life. He used the battles as the tools to spread his message. Whenever he confronted the enemies, he invited his adversaries towards Islam and persuaded them from shedding the blood of the people. As a matter of fact he was not a king, Monarch, Emperor or Ruler of any State but essentially the messenger of God who had come on earth as a mercy upon mankind to lead them on the path of piety and good moral conduct and not to fight wars and kill people.

Another important thing in connection with the wars that the Guide of Islam fought was that he did not use any superior technology to defeat his enemies as had been the practice in the world since the wars were invented. The experience reveals that those savages who discovered the use of fire or the art of stitching or the power of wheel succeeded in conquering those who were unaware of them. Likewise, those who invented arrows successfully enslaved those who were living in Stone Age. Similarly, those who entered into the agricultural era proved far superior over those who were dependent upon mere hunting. In the same way, those who tamed horses or used elephants crushed those soldiers on war fronts who were fighting on the strength of their limbs. Human records testify to the fact that with the invention and discovery of copper and iron the fates of many nations were severely affected. Those who used guns and cannons against those who used swords turned out to be triumphant. The whole fate of World War II was changed in favour of allied forces merely due to dropping of two atom bombs on Nagasaki and Hiroshima. United States of America, U.K., Germany, France, Israel and Japan etc. are at a privileged position despite their low numerical strength compared to big and most populated countries because of their superior technologies.

When the Ruler of Islam confronted the enemies who had invaded him with soldiers equipped with swords, spears and horses, he did not equip his soldiers with new tools to fight the adversaries but provided them the technology of faith. He convinced them that the victories and defeats were in the hands of God only and assured them that since they were fighting in the way of God their victories were certain. His followers believed in what he preached and found every word and sentence true as he said. He completely transformed the characters, conducts and behaviour patterns of his soldiers with the spirit of Islam and imbibed in them that courage and confidence which the world had never seen among any warriors on any battle field in the world. His warriors dauntlessly ran over deserts, plateaus, mountains and jungles; triumphantly crossed rivers, lakes, seas and oceans; did not bother about scorching heat, shivering cold, thundering clouds and dark nights and clashed fearlessly with the mightiest kingdoms, majestic emperors, splendid kings, powerful monarchs and renowned chiefs. They never fought any war for worldly gains but fought all wars in the name of God that were imposed upon them. They followed the principles of truth, justice and never abandoned them even on the battle fields as well as after the wars were over. They had firm faith that those who were martyred on the battle fields or returned victorious in the cause of Allah had their immense rewards with their Lord. It was because of the teachings of the Genius of Islam that his three hundred and thirteen soldiers defeated one thousand strong Quraish at Badr and one thousand compelled the three thousand fighters at Uhud to flee and his three thousand humiliated ten thousand soldiers at the Battle of Trench. Not only this, his three thousand soldiers clashed with two hundred thousand Byzantine soldiers at Syria without caring for their lives. Thus, with the spirit of faith and belief in One true God, he provided so much power and strength to his soldiers that his adversaries were compelled to surrender before him as Hitler and Mussolini surrendered before Churchill and Roosevelt in the Second World War.

NOTES

1. Shafiur Rahman al-Mubarakpuri, op. cit., p. 323.
2. Abdul Hameed Siddiqui, op. cit., p. 229.
3. Shafiur Rahman al-Mubarakpuri, op. cit., p. 343.
4. Ahmad A. Zidan, op. cit., p. 184.
5. Abdul Hameed Siddiqui, op. cit., p. 255.
6. *Ibid.*, p. 161.
7. *Ibid.*, p. 174.
8. *Ibid.*, p. 176.
9. *Ibid.*, p. 178.

6

The Peaceful Efforts of the Ruler of Islam to Spread his Message

The Prophet of Islam was deputed by God to spread the message of true God among those people who had gone astray. He never wanted to propagate any ism or ideology or any dogma or system upon people. Likewise, he was not interested in worldly charms, material benefits or name and fame. Besides, he was least interested in imposing his religion upon people by force and he never approved the idea that people accepted his religion under duress or it was imposed upon them against their sweet will. Similarly, he was not at all interested in the territories, properties and possessions of others and never wanted to destabilize kingdoms, terrorize people, shed their blood and subjugate them for his personal benefits. He simply wanted the facility to convey his message to the people so that they might decide for themselves what was good for them. It was his misfortune that the Emperors, Kings, Monarchs, Rulers, Chiefs and the Leaders of his times did not allow him to preach his message among their people. They were so afraid of him that they did not want to see that he met their people for they were convinced that he would win over them to his point of view. They not only threatened him and stopped him from spreading his message but punished and brutalized those who went towards him. Many of them killed his envoys, several caused severe injuries to his ambassadors and there was no dearth of people who stopped his messengers by force from entering within their territories. The main difficulty with him was that he did not have other means at his disposal to propagate his mission as are presently available in modern times. He was compelled by the responsibilities of the task imposed upon him by God to send his people to those who were misguided despite immense risk to their lives. He was fully conscious of his responsibilities that he owed to mankind as the Last Messenger of God. He knew that he was sent on the earth not merely to guide people according to the God-given principles but was also deputed as the Mercy upon whole mankind and hence he was duty bound to spread the message of Islam among all those people of the world who were not aware of it. After reaching Medina he could not spread his message effectively among the people living nearby Medina because he was mostly busy in fighting the aggressive designs of the Quraish.

THROUGH LETTERS AND ENVOYS TO KINGS, EMPERORS AND MONARCHS

When he got a heaven-sent opportunity provided by the Treaty of Al-Hudaibiyah, he turned his attention to address other Emperors, Kings, Rulers, Nobles and Chiefs beyond Arabia and sent his envoys to deliver to them the message of the All-pervasive and All-pervading Allah. Once he addressed his companions by saying that he was sent as a blessing to all mankind to carry the message of Islam to all corners of the world and it was the duty of his companions to help him and neither to differ nor to deter as the disciples of Prophet Jesus did who were sent afar and were thereby punished by Lord. He selected his envoys on the basis of their knowledge, experience, wisdom, genius and aptitude. In order to provide authenticity to their credentials a silver seal was made on which was engraved the words "Muhammad the Messenger of Allah" in the following order in Arabic:

Allah
Rasool (Messenger)
Muhammad

ENVOY TO HERACLIUS, THE EMPEROR OF BYZANTINES

In 629 the Ruler of Islam sent letters and courier to the Kings of Persia, Yemen, Ethiopia and to the Emperor Heraclius to convey to them the message of Islam. First of all he sent Diyah bin Khalifa Kalbi as his envoy to Heraclius, the Emperor of Byzantines. Al-Bukhari gave a long detail about the letter sent to him. Diyah Kalbi delivered the letter of the Ruler of Islam to Heraclius who had come to Jerusalem to celebrate his victory over Persia. He was presented before the Emperor after several ceremonies. Before delivering the letter, Diyah Kalbi gave an introductory speech as under:

"O Caesar of Rome! The one who has deputed me as an ambassador to you is more exalted than your gracious highness and the Mighty Lord has sent him to us as the Messenger and the Greatest of all. Please listen to me with earnest attention and give me a solemn reply. If you do not pay full attention you may not reach to its true meanings and if your reply does not come out from the core of your heart justice would not have been done to it. O mighty King! You know it well that Jesus, the son of Mary offered prayers." Since the King had replied in affirmative, he continued by saying, "I then invite you to the Magnificent Lord, to whom Jesus offered prayers, prostrated before him and who shaped him in the womb of Mary and who created the heavens and the earth. Then I invite you to that Prophet who received no formal education and whose advent was foretold by Moses and Jesus and you are completely aware of these facts. If you accept his message you would be immensely rewarded in this world as well as hereafter. However, if you do not accept it you would be deprived of all the blessings. Believe me, there is only One All-pervading Lord who penalizes the disbelievers and changes their fortunes."[1] On hearing this, Heraclius called Abu Sufyan who by that time had not embraced Islam and asked him several questions about the Holy Prophet and his religion. Strangely, the reply that Abu Sufyan provided to him about the truthful and the trustworthy personality of the Guardian of Islam and his religion which was doing immense good to mankind puzzled and perplexed the king. Finally the following letter of the Prophet was read loudly before the audiences:

> "In the name of Allah, the most Beneficent, the Most Merciful.

This letter is from Muhammad, the slave of Allah and His Messenger to Heraclius, the Emperor of Rome.

Blessed are indeed those who follow the true guidance. I invite you to come within the fold of Islam. If you do this you would be safe and secure. If you embrace Islam, God will bless you with double reward, but if you turn your back upon it then the burden of the sins of all your people shall fall upon your shoulders.

O people of the Scripture! Come to a word that is common between us and you, that we shall worship none but Allah and that we shall associate no partners with him, and that none of us shall take others as lords besides Allah. Then, if they turn away, say: Bear witness that we are Muslims."[2]

Having heard the contents of the letter and the observations of Abu Sufyan about the Prophet of God and Islam the king was highly impressed but his positive reaction created tension among the clergy in the court and Heraclius did not embrace Islam because it was differently ordained. However, the envoy returned to Medina with ample gifts, presents and felicitations from the king. Unfortunately Dihayah Al-Kalbi was intercepted at Hasmi while returning to Medina by a tribe from Judhan and they looted the presents sent to the Prophet. Zaid bin Haritha heading five hundred warriors caused heavy casualties upon the enemy and returned with 1000 camels, 5000 cattle and several prisoners. Since the chief of Judham had embraced Islam and had complained to Holy Prophet about his fate, the Guide of Islam ordered that all the spoils and his captives be returned to him.

LETTER TO CHOSROES, THE EMPEROR OF PERSIA

Soon after this, another letter bearing the same seal and with more or less similar matter was sent with Abdullah bin Hudhafa As-Sahmi to Chosroes, the Emperor of Persia. The contents of the letter were as follows:

"In the name of Allah, the Most Beneficent and Most Merciful.

From Muhammad, the Messenger of Allah to Chosroes, King of Persia. Peace be upon him who follows true guidance, believes in Allah and His Messenger and certifies that there is no god save Allah, the Alone with no partners and that Muhammad is His slave and Messenger. I invite you to embrace the religion of Allah. I am the Messenger of Allah sent to all people in order that I may infuse fear of Allah in every living person, and that the charge may be proved against those who reject the truth. Accept Islam as your religion so that you may live in safety, otherwise you will be responsible for all the sins of the Magians."[3]

The arrogant Emperor was highly irritated by the contents and the style of the letter as well as with the fact that the name of Holy Prophet was written before his name. He could not tolerate the insult caused upon him and became so angry that out of a fit of anger he tore the letter of the Ruler of Islam into pieces and forthwith ordered his viceroy at Yemen to send soldiers to arrest the Holy Prophet and present him in his court. The governor Bazan immediately sent two persons to Medina for the purpose. When the dirty reaction of Chosroes was communicated to Holy Prophet by his envoy Abdullah bin Hudhayfah, the Ruler of Islam smiled and said "Allah will rend and scatter his kingdom into pieces in the same way as he has torn my letter." As soon as the men of Bazan reached Medina Lord informed the Holy Prophet that the King was killed by his own son. Holy Prophet disclosed this news to the enemy soldiers and they were dumb founded. They rushed back and there they found that Parvez had been assassinated by his own son and he had captured the entire kingdom. Bazan embraced Islam and whole-heartedly surrendered along with his paraphernalia before the Exalted Highness of Islam.

MESSAGE TO NEGUS, THE KING OF ABYSSINIA

Abyssinia (Ethiopia) was a different country those days. It was ruled by a pious and kind Christian ruler named Ashama bin As-Famari or Negus the King of Abyssinia. He had provided shelter to Jafar and his companions who on the advice of Holy Prophet had migrated from Makkah to Abyssinia. The King did not handover the Muslims to chiefs of Makkah despite their several requests and persuasions. The Guardian of Islam had a soft corner for Negus because of his helping the Muslims in distress and his kind behaviour towards his subjects. The letter was delivered by Amr bin Omaiyah Ad-Damari and the details of the letter were as follows:

"In the name of Allah, the Most Compassionate and Most Merciful,

This letter is from Muhammad the Apostle of God to Negus, the King of Abyssinia. Salutations.

Glory be to Allah, there is no god but He, the Sovereign, the Holy, the Provider of Safety, the source of tranquility, the Giver of Peace, the Protector of faith, and the Mighty. I bear witness that Jesus, the son of Mary, is the spirit of Allah and his Word which He cast into Mary, the Virgin, the good, the pure, so that she conceived Jesus. Allah created him from His spirit and His breathing as He created Adam by his Hand. I call you to Allah Alone, without any associate and to his obedience and to follow me and to believe in that which came to me, for I am the Messenger of Allah. I invite you and your men to the God, the Greatest and the Mightiest. I hereby bear witness that I have communicated my message and advice. I invite you to listen and accept my advice. Peace be upon him who follows true guidance."[4]

The King received 'Amr bin Omaiyah As-Damari the envoy of the Prophet with great respect. He descended the floor, placed the letter on his eyes and confessed his faith in Islam. He gave the following most respectful reply and regretted his inability to personally present himself at the feet of the Holy Prophet:

"In the name of Allah, the Most Beneficent, the Most Merciful,

From Negus Ashama to Muhammad, the Messenger of Allah. Peace be upon you O Messenger of Allah! And mercy and blessing from Allah beside Whom there is no god. I have received your letter in which you have mentioned about Jesus and by the Lord of heaven and earth, Jesus is no more than what you say. We fully acknowledge that with which you have been sent to us and we have entertained your cousin and his companions. I bear witness that you are the Messenger of God, true and confirming (those who have gone before you). I pledge to you through your cousin and surrender myself through him to the Lord of the worlds." Negus died shortly after the Battle of Tabuk but he sent Ja'far and his companions back home as directed by Holy Prophet. He was succeeded by another king to whom was also written a letter by the Ruler of Islam but nobody knows whether he accepted Islam or not.

LETTER TO MUQAWQAS, THE VICEGERENT OF EGYPT

Hatib bin Abi Balta'a was sent to Egypt to deliver the letter of Holy Prophet to Muqawqas, the Vicegerent of Egypt and Alexandria. He requested for an audience with Muqawqas and before delivering the letter addressed him by saying that there used to be someone before him who tried to downgrade the status of the Lord hence he was humiliated and badly punished in his life and was made an example in the Hereafter. One should take heed from it for it is always unwise to set the bad example for others. The Vicegerent replied that he was not prepared to leave his religion till he found a better one. Hatib then said that he invited him to embrace Islam which would suffice him all that he might lose. His Prophet had called people to profess Islam but the Quraish and Jews stood against him as bitter enemies but Christians stood closest to his call. Moses's news about Christ was identical to the latter's good tidings about the advent of Muhammad. Likewise, his invitation to him to embrace Islam was similar to their invitation to people of Torah to accept the New Testament. He was not dissuading him from his religion but bidding him to adhere to its tenets, with the proviso that once a prophet emerges in a nation, he is eligible for positive response and everyone becomes subject to the same divine law. Muqawqas read the contents of the letter thoroughly, mediated over it and replied that he was convinced that the Prophet of Islam was none but one who possessed all the symptoms of prophethood.

He kept the letter in the ivory casket and promised to consider the matter deeply.

The contents of the letter of Holy Prophet were as under:

> "In the name of Allah, the Most Beneficent, the Most Merciful,

From Muhammad, the slave of Allah and His Messenger, to Muqawqas, Vicegerent of Egypt.

Peace be upon him who follows true guidance. Thereafter, I call you to embrace Islam. Therefore, if you want security, accept Islam. If you embrace Islam, Allah, the Almighty, shall bless you doubly. But if you reject it, you will face the burden of the transgression of all the Copts. O people of the Scripture, come to a word that is just between us and you, that we worship none but Allah, and that we associate no partners to Him, and that none of us shall take others as lords besides Allah." Then, if they turn away, say, "Bear witness that we are Muslims".[5]

Muqawqas gave the following reply:

> "In the name of Allah, the Most Beneficent, the Most Merciful,

From Muqawqas to Muhammad bin 'Abdullah.

Peace be upon you. I have read your letter and understood its contents, and what you are calling for. I already know that the coming of a Prophet is still due, but I used to believe he would be born in Syria. I am sending you as presents two maids, who come from noble Coptic families, clothing and a steed for riding on. Peace be upon you."[6]

Muqawqas did not accept Islam but his presents were accepted by Holy Prophet. As a token of friendship Maria, the first maid was taken by the Ruler of Islam in his marriage and she gave birth to his son Ibrahim and Sirin, the other maid was given to Hassan bin Thabit As-Ansari.

A LETTER TO MUNDHIR BIN SAWA, GOVERNOR OF BAHRAIN

Holy Prophet sent Al-'Ala bin Al-Haramin to Al-Mundhir bin Sawa, Governor of Bahrain carrying his letter asking him to embrace Islam. He replied as under:

> Peace be upon Allah's Messenger. I received your injunctions. Prior to this, I read your letter, which you wrote to the people of Bahrain extending to them an invitation to Islam. Islam appealed to some of them and they entered the fold of Islam, while others did not find it appealing. In my opinion there live Magians and Jews and therefore you may inform me of the treatment to be extended to them.

Holy Prophet gave the following reply:

> "In the name of Allah, the Most Beneficent, the Most Merciful.

From Muhammad, the Messenger of Allah to Mundhir bin Sawa. Peace be on you! I praise Allah with no associate and I bear witness that Muhammad is His slave and Messenger.

Thereafter, I remind you of Allah, the Great, the Glorious.

Whoever accepts admonition does it for his own good. Whoever follows my messengers and acts in accordance with their guidance, he, in fact, accepts my advice.

My messengers have highly praised your behaviour. You shall continue in your present office. Give the new Muslims full chance to preach the religion. I accept your recommendation regarding the people of Bahrain and I pardon the offences of the offenders; therefore, you may also forgive them.

Of the people of Bahrain whoever wants to go on in their Jewish or Magian faith, should be made to pay Jizya (poll-tax)."[7]

LETTER TO HAUDHA BIN 'ALI, GOVERNOR OF YAMAMA

Holy Prophet sent Sulait bin Amr Al-'Amiri to Haudha bin Ali, Governor of Yamama with the following letter:

"In the name of Allah, the Most Beneficent, the Most Merciful,

From Muhammad, Messenger of Allah to Haudha bin 'Ali, Governor of Yamama. Peace be upon him who follows true guidance. Be informed that my religion shall prevail everywhere. You should accept Islam, and whatever under your command shall remain yours."

Haudha bin 'Ali replied in following tone:

"The faith to which you invite me, is very good. I am a famous orator and poet, the Arabs highly respect me and I am of account among them. If you include me in your government, I am prepared to follow you."[8] Haudha conferred a reward on Muslim envoy Sulait bin 'Amr Al-'Amiri and presented him with clothes made of Hair fabric which were deposited by the envoy in the trust of the Holy Prophet. The Prophet of Islam did not accept his condition and left the matter to Almighty God. Later on Gabriel came with the revelation that Haudha was dead. While communicating this information to the people the Holy Prophet also told them that Yamama would produce a liar who will arrogate Prophethood to himself but would subsequently be killed, which proved to be correct.

LETTER TO HARITH BIN ABI SHAMIR AL-GHASSANI, KING OF DAMASCUS

Holy Prophet sent a communication through Shuja' bin Wahab to Harith bin Abi Shamir Al-Ghassani, the King of Damascus with following contents:

> "In the name of Allah. The Most Beneficent, the Most Merciful.

From Muhammad, Messenger of Allah to Al-Harith bin Abi Shamir, the King of Damascus.

Peace be upon him who follows true guidance, believes it and regards it as true. I invite you to believe in Allah Alone with no associate, thence after your kingdom will remain yours."[9]

When the letter was read in the audience of the King, he became furious and rejected the offer to come within the fold of Islam and cried in the fit of anger that he would fight those who would try to dispose him of his throne.

LETTER TO THE KING OF 'OMAN, JAIFER, AND HIS BROTHER ABD AL-JALANDI

'Amr bin al-'As was deputed by the Prophet of Islam to carry his following letter to Jaifer and his brother:

> "In the name of Allah, the Most Beneficent, the Most Merciful.

From Muhammad bin 'Abdullah to Jaifer, and his brother, Abd Al-Jalandi. Peace be upon him who follows true guidance; thereafter I invite both of you to the fold of Islam. Accept Islam, Allah has sent me as a Prophet to all His creatures in order that I may instill fear of Allah in the hearts of His disobedient creatures so that there may be left no excuse for those who deny Allah. If you embrace Islam, you will remain in command of your country, but if you refuse my offer you have got to remember that all your possessions are perishable."[10]

Jaifer after much persuasion and on the advice of his younger brother Abd Al-Jalandi embraced Islam and the frontiers of Islam extended to new areas. The Holy Prophet successfully managed to spread the message of Islam among the Kings, Emperors and Monarchs of those times through his polite, precise and meaningful letters. Some of them embraced Islam, a few developed soft corner towards it while others remained within the fold of their own faith but the idea of accepting Islam and the emergence of the last Prophet of God always remained heavy on their necks.

UNIQUENESS OF HIS LETTERS

The Ruler of Arabian Peninsula wrote several letters a few of which we have mentioned above. They were simple, polite, humble, precise, straightforward, meaningful and full of confidence as the Holy Prophet himself was. They reflected every trait of his magnificent personality. Just as he was unique, unmatchable and exemplary so also were his letters. The historians have seen innumerable letters written by the Kings and emperors but they cannot sight a single letter matching to the beautiful and highly appealing letters of the Ruler of Islam. The arrogant, boastful and threatening letters of several hot-headed Emperors, despotic kings and cruel Rulers either reflected their vanities, pride, egos and magnanimity or expressed their angers, hatred and enmity. They were in no way constructive and reformative in nature and beneficial and helpful to mankind. They either talked of severing heads, destroying kingdoms, shedding blood, taking revenge or pertained to giving titles, bestowing favours or glorifying their names, fames, dignities and grandeurs. They were very often written in golden letters on embroidered silken parchments and sent through the gorgeous envoys. They began with the praise, glory, exaltedness, highness and magnificence of the kings who sent the letters and ended equating them to the Lord of the worlds. The subject matter revolved merely around the subjugation and surrender to the wills of the kingly desires and there was no mention of grace and glory of the Lord and need for material, moral and spiritual advancement. As against this, if one looks at the contents, style and tone of the letters of the Ruler of Islam one is bound to confess that indeed they were very simple, convincing, meaningful, vibrant and full of confidence. They had nothing to do with the dignity, grace and personal life of the Holy Prophet. So also they did not revolve around whims, desires, worldly matters, threats, favours or personal likings and disliking of the Ruler of Islam. They were neither studded in gold and silver nor were written on silken parchments nor were sent through glamorous envoys but were written on simple material and delivered by the innocent, pious, meaningful and highly straightforward and pious people.

Despite being one of the Greatest Rulers of his time, he never called himself Emperor or King or Ruler but simply Muhammad (PBUH) the slave and the Messenger of God. He neither criticized the functioning, style of working or behaviour pattern nor religion or ideology of any Emperor, King, Ruler or Noble but highlighted the truth, usefulness and the necessity of worshipping one true God. Without attacking the belief systems of Jews, Christians, Magians, Sabians and polytheists he invited them towards Islam being the true religion of God. He neither threatened any king nor threw any challenge nor posed any problem before the rulers but showed them the true path and assured them of better future in this world as well as hereafter. He did not try to project himself as a great man or a statesman or genius but submitted himself as humble, meek and truthful Warner. Likewise, he did not use Islam to enhance his prestige and significance but projected it merely as the panacea for all ills of the society. He remained precise, to the point and never tried to discuss irrelevant and unnecessary matters. He tried his best that no controversial, dissenting or objectionable matter was raised so as to create any ill-will in between him and the others. Besides, he never invited the Kings, Monarchs, Rulers and Emperors towards something new or revolutionary and towards values which were common between him and them. His letters were not political, diplomatic and personal but missionary, purposive and eye openers, thought-provoking and conscience awakening.

It is worth noting that Holy Prophet neither considered the spread of Islam as an expansionist movement launched by a political personality for self aggrandizement nor treated it as a weapon of power politics. It was projected as a divine mission and hence the question of sharing of power or winning people by various baits or peoples putting various conditions to join Islam did not arise. It was an endeavour which wanted an unconditional surrender of one's self not before him but before one's Creator. The whole theme of the letters was that Only One true God was the God of all people, Holy Prophet was merely the Messenger of God and Islam was the true religion in which all the previous prophets believed and human progress, prosperity and peace lied only in moving on the path shown by Islam. Over and above this, it was also emphasized that if Islam was to be accepted as a code of conduct and way of life it was to be embraced with complete sincerity and devotion strictly on its own merit and not due to any fear, compulsion or worldly considerations. Moreover, history also testifies to this fact that when the letters of the Kings, Emperors and Monarchs were received with disrespect or their envoys were ill-treated wars were inevitable. However, the Ruler of Islam did not react violently but prayed in their favour and urged the Lord to give them proper guidance.

HE REACHED PEOPLE THROUGH HIS SERMONS AND SPEECHES

It will not be out of place to mention here that he did not take the support of mere letters but also taught principles of Islam to people everyday in the Mosques, in the markets, in huts and in villages. He took the risk of meeting the heads of various tribes within their own jurisdictions outside Medina and sent several delegations to other tribes living far from Medina with a view to bring them within the fold of Islam. He received many delegations that came to him for his guidance and confronted different individuals in their dwellings, residences, and places of work and convinced them of the utility of Islam. He gave sermons even on the battle fields before actual start of war and tried his best to dissuade people from shedding each other's blood. The lecture that the Ruler of Islam gave at Tabuk to his troops after seeing that his adversaries had fled was wonderful.

His speech was entirely different from those given by various wining and conquering Kings, Monarchs and Emperors. In his speech he neither boasted about his power, prestige and grandeur nor praised the bravery of his troops nor humiliated his enemies nor incited his troops to loot and plunder but invited their attention towards basics of civilized society. He Praised almighty God and profusely thanked Him and said:

"Well, surely the most truthful exposition is the Book of God. The highly reliable support is the deed of piety. The extremely trustworthy religion is the religion of Abraham. The best of precedents is the Sunna (practice) of Muhammad. The grandest invocation is the Utterance of Allah. The noblest of the narratives is Qur'an. The most praiseworthy affairs are those that are based on sane consensus. The worst things in religion are those which are done without sanction. The most note worthy path is that followed by the Prophets. The adorable death is that of the martyrs. The most painful ignorance is the waywardness after guidance. The most useful actions are those that are beneficial. The best guidance is that which is put into practice. The most hopeless blindness is the blindness of the heart. The upper hand is superior to the lower hand. The little that provides contentment is better than abundant and alluring. The worst apology is that which is submitted having seen the angel of death. The worst remorse is that which would be felt on the Day of Reckoning. Some people attend Friday prayer hesitatingly and causing delay. Some of them remember Allah but reluctantly. The tongue which is used to falsehood is the bubbling source of the sins. The most valuable possession is the contentment of the heart. The best provision is that of righteousness. The grandest wisdom is the fear of Allah, the Mighty, the Great. The best thing to cherish in the hearts is the faith and conviction; doubt is nothing but infidelity.

Impatient wailing and fulsome laudation of the dead is the act of the days of ignorance. Betrayal leads one to the fire of hell. Drinking amounts to burning. Obscene poetry is the handy made of the devils. Wine is the mother of all evils. The worst thing that can be eaten is that which belongs to the orphans. Blessed indeed is place of four cubit. Your affairs would be finally decided in the next life. The false dream is the worst dream. Whatever is in store is to happen soon. To abuse the believer is crossing the limits; raising arms against him is deceit. To backbite him is the disobedience of Allah. Inviolability of his property is like that of his blood. He who falsely swears in the name of Allah actually falsifies Him. He pardons others would himself be granted pardon. He who forgives others, Allah would forgive his sins. He who suppresses anger, Allah rewards him. He who faces misfortunes with perseverance, Allah compensates him. He who works only for name and fame, Allah disgraces him. He who shows patience and forgiveness, Allah gives him a double reward. He who disobeys Allah, Allah chastises him.

I seek the forgiveness of Allah.
I seek the forgiveness of Allah.
I seek the forgiveness of Allah."[11]

The above speech of the Commander of Islam was entirely different from all the speeches given by any Emperor, King, Monarch, Dictator, Commander, Conqueror or Chief to his troops anywhere, anytime, on any part of the earth. The above speech was delivered by him when he was at Tabuk and was heading a mighty troop of thirty thousand warriors and had reached there after crossing several hurdles. Besides, his enemies were conspicuous by absence having heard his arrival. In a sense it was a victory speech. It should have been full of his pride, ego, vanity, glory, courage, leadership and bravery as well as the valour, dauntlessness and unmatching power of his warriors but it appears that there was not an iota of that in this speech.

From the above speech it appears that the Ruler of Islam neither had his eyes on the territories, kingdoms, booties and wealth and possessions of his rivals nor wanted to make them slaves, refugees, captives and subjugated. If that was the case none could stop him from capturing the rich surroundings of Syria which lay undefended at his feet. His basic purpose was to bring people from darkness to light. His main aim was to remove their evils, reform their anti-social and inhuman habits and cultivate in them the piety, compassion and exemplary conducts. All his energies and efforts were directed towards a single end of guiding people on the right path. Whatever he thought, whatever he planned and whatever he did were the outcome of his keen desire that mankind recognize their true Creator and move on the guidance provided by Him and surrender before His commandments wholeheartedly. Alexander, the great did not do it, Cyrus, the mighty, never practiced it, Constantine, the gracious remained away from it and Peter, the majestic never made it a part of his state policy. Genghis Khan swallowed the territories of the people, Hitler invaded countries after countries, Napoleon had his eyes on the surrounding kingdoms, Caesar was hungry of power and William, the conqueror always used the sword to subdue people. The purpose to write his letters was that the Ruler of Islam wanted to convince the people that he was neither a plunderer nor conqueror nor hungry for power nor like the worldly Emperors, Monarchs, Kings and Rulers but he was a unique personality never seen before. Just as he revolutionized the whole pattern of living of the believers in Medina on sound moral and secular principles so also he wanted to rationalize the obscured and barbarous notions and ways of living of Arabs and non-Arabs during wars and peace on humanistic norms and ideal principles laid down by God.

HE MET THE TRIBES AND CONFRONTED THE INDIVIDUALS

His peaceful approach can be judged from the fact that when Makkans discarded him, he visited Ta'if and when the people of Ta'if did not heed him, he did not lose hope but met different tribes at the time of pilgrimage at Makkah since the fourth year of his Prophet hood and introduced to them the utility and the usefulness of Islam. According to reliable sources Islam was introduced to Banu 'Amir bin Sa'aa'ah, Muharib bin Khasfa, Banu Al-Buka, Al-Harith bin Ka'b, Fazatah, Ghassan, Murrah, Haneefah, Saleem, Abs, Banu Nasr Kindah, Kalb and Udhrah but they did not accept it. He approached a segment of Banu Kalb or Banu Abdullah and invited them towards Islam but in vain. From Banu Haneefah also he did not receive any encouraging reply. He went to the encampment of Bani 'Amr bin Sa'aa'ah and addressed them there but found very little response from their sides. He was not disheartened and talked to individual people. For instance, he met Swaid bin Samit a poet from Medina at the time of the eleventh year of his prophethood while he was at Makkah for lesser pilgrimage and he gladly embraced Islam. Similarly, Evas bin Mu'adh, a young lad who had come with the delegation to Makkah to seek the help of the Quraish against Al-Khajraj was moved by the wisdom of the Holy Prophet and came gladly within the fold of Islam though he died no sooner than he reached Medina. In the same way, Abu Shar Al-Ghifari who lived in the suburbs of Medina accepted openly Islam, though Holy Prophet had forbidden him to do so and for which he was beaten severely by the opponents of Islam. It was due to the intervention of Al-Abbas that he was saved. Tufail bin 'Amr Ad-dausi a poet and chief of Ad-Daus tribe living close to Yemen in south Arabia also embraced Islam when he visited

Makkah in the eleventh year of the Prophethood of Islam. When the Quraish told him many adverse things about the Holy Prophet and advised him not to meet him, he met the Prophet per chance and he was so impressed that he got converted to Islam and persuaded his father, wife and others to embrace Islam which they ultimately did. Dhumad Al-Azdi belonged to Azd Shanu'a in Yemen and he practiced incantation. He had heard many things about the Holy Prophet but when he met him he neither found him poet nor soothsayer nor sorcerer but the Messenger of God and embraced Islam. It was in the eleventh year of his Prophethood that six people from Khazraj tribe of Medina namely As'ad bin Zurarah, 'Awf bin Harith, Rafi' bin Malik, Qutbah bin 'Amir, Uqbah bin 'Amr and Jabir bin Abdullah got converted to Islam and spread Islam at Medina when they visited the town.

SENT SEVERAL DELEGATIONS

After coming from Ta'if, the Ruler of Islam received several delegations from far off places and dispatched delegations to several tribes under the command of able and learned people with a view to guide them on the path of Islam. In the ninth year of Al-Hijra, the Guide of Islam sent the following delegations to the tribes named therein:

1. Uyaina bin Hisn to Bani Tamim,
2. Yazeed bin Husain to Aslam and Ghifar,
3. 'Abbad bin Bishar Al-Ashhali to Sulaiam and Muzainah,
4. Rafi' bin Mukaith to Juhainah,
5. 'Amr bin Al-'As to bani Fazatah,
6. Ad-Dahhak bin Sufyan to Bini Kilab,
7. Basher bin Sufyan to Bani Ka'b,
8. Ibn Al-lutabiyah Al-Azdi to Bani Dhubyan,
9. Al-Muhajir bin Abi Omaiyah to sana'a' (Al-Aswad Al-'Ansi called at him when he was in it.),
10. Ziyad bin Labid to hadramout,
11. 'adi bin hatim to Tai' and Bani Asad,

12. Malik bin Nuwairah to Bani hanzalah,
13. Az-Zabraqan bin Badr to Bani Sa'd (a portion of them),
14. Qais bin 'asim to Bani Sa'd (a portion of them),
15. Al-'Ala' bin Al—Hadrami to Al-Bahrain,
16. Ali-bin Abi Talib to Najran (to collect Sadaqa & Jijya)[12]

The above delegations proved successful in the end and all of the tribes embraced Islam voluntarily.

FAREWELL PILGRIMAGE SPEECH

His peaceful approach and the sincerity of purpose can be inferred from the fact that when he was in his sixty-third year of his life which coincided with the tenth year of Hijrah, he had realized that he was to meet his Lord soon because his mission was complete as people were coming within the fold of Islam caravan after caravan in multitudes. He, therefore, decided to perform his last pilgrimage called 'Farewell Pilgrimage' with more than 114,000 Muslims including his wives. On the 9th of Dhul Hijjah after Morning Prayer he delivered the following speech at Arafat after glorifying God before hundred thousand twenty-four or hundred thousand and forty-four people:

"O People! Listen to what I say for I do not know whether I will ever meet you at this place once again after this current year. O People! Verily your blood, your property and your honour are sacred and inviolable until you appear before your Lord, as this day and this month is sacred for all. Verily you will meet your Lord and you will be held answerable for your actions. Have I not conveyed the message? O Allah be my witness.

He who has any trust with him he should restore it to the person who deposited it with him.

Beware, no one committing a crime is responsible for it but he himself. Neither the son is responsible for the crime of his father, nor the father is responsible for the crime of his son.

O People! Listen to my words and understand them. You must know that a Muslim is the brother of the Muslim and they form one brotherhood. Nothing of his brother is lawful for a Muslim except what he himself allows willingly. So you should not oppress one another. O Allah! Have I not conveyed the message?

Behold! All practices of paganism and ignorance are now under my feet. The blood-revenges of the days of Ignorance are remitted. The first claim on blood I abolish is that of Ibn Rabi'ah who was nursed in the tribe of Sa'd and whom the Hudhayl killed.

Usury is forbidden but you will be entitled to recover your principal. Wrong not and you would not be wronged. Allah has decreed that there should be no usury and I make a beginning by remitting the amount of interest which Abbas b. 'Abd al Mttalib has to receive. Verily it is remitted entirely.

O People! I fear Allah concerning women. Verily you have taken them on the security of Allah and have made their persons lawful unto you by words of Allah! Verily you have got certain rights over your women and your women have certain rights over you. It is incumbent upon them to honour their conjugal rights and, not commit acts of impropriety which if they do, you have authority to chastise them, yet not severely. If your wives refrain from impropriety and are faithful to you, clothe and feed them suitably. Behold! Lay injunctions upon women but kindly.

O People! Verily Allah has ordained to every man the share of his inheritance. The child belongs to the marriage-bed and the violator of wedlock shall be stoned. He who attributes his ancestry to other than his father or claims his client ship to other than his masters, the curse of Allah, that of the angels, and of the people be upon him. Allah will accept from him neither repentance nor righteousness.

O People! Verily the Satan is disappointed at being ever worshipped in this land of yours, but he can be obeyed in anything short of worship he will be pleased in matters you may be disposed to think of little account, so beware of him in your matters of religion.

Verily, I have left amongst you the Book of Allah and the Sunnah (practices of the Holy Prophet) of His Apostle which if you hold fast, you shall never go astray.

"And if you were asked about me, what would you say?"

They replied: "We bear witness that you have conveyed the message and discharged your ministry."[13]

Next day the Prophet of Islam continued his speech after the praise of the Lord repeating some of the salient points of the previous speech and highlighting a few new matters as under:

> O People! Verily the intercalation (of a prohibited month) aggravates infidelity. Thereby the unbelievers are led to wrong. For they make it lawful one year and forbid it in another year to be in conformity with the number (of months) which Allah declared unlawful so they consider violable that which Allah declared to be inviolable and they consider inviolable what Allah declared to be violable.

Verily the time has revolved in its own way from the day when the heavens and the earth were created. The number of months to Allah is twelve of which four are sacred; three are consecutive—Dhul Qa'da, Dhul Hijjah, Muhattam, and Rajab which is between Jumadah and Sha'ban.

O People! Do you know what day it is, what territory it is, what month it is?

To this the people answered: The day is the day of sacrifice; and the territory is the sacred territory, the month is the sacred month. At each reply he said:

So I apprise you that your lives, your property and your honour must be sacred to one another as this sacred day, in this sacred month, in this sacred town.

And your slaves! See that you feed them with such food as you eat yourselves and clothe them with the clothes that you yourselves wear. And if they commit a fault which you are not inclined to forgive, then part with them for they are the servants of Allah and are not be chastised.

Behold! Listen to me. Worship your Lord, offer prayers five times a day; observe fast in the month of Ramadan; make pilgrimage to the House (Ka'bah); pay readily the zakat (poor-due) on your property and obey whatever I command you, only then you will get into the heaven.

"Let him that is present convey it unto him who is absent. For happily, many people to whom the message is conveyed may be more mindful of it then the audience."

He continued his oratory the next day too and emphasized as follows:

> O People! Verily your Lord is one and your father is one. All of men belong to one ancestry of Adam and Adam was created out of clay. There is no superiority for an Arab over a non-Arab and for a non-Arab over Arab. Nor for white over the black nor for the black over the white except in piety, 'verily the noblest among you is he who is the most pious.' (xlix: 13)

Behold, the nearer ones of you should convey the message to the remoter ones. I have conveyed the message. Then looking up to the heaven, he said:

> O Lord! I have delivered the message and discharged my ministry.
>
> Yes. Cried all the people crowding round him, "Yes, verily you have.

"O Lord! I beseech Thee bear Thou witness unto it." With these narrations the Ruler of Islam completed his address at the time of his "Last Farewell pilgrimage" which turned out be really the last, for the Gracious Ruler of Islam left the world the same year as he had told the people while delivering his speech.[14]

See the sincerity and the commitment of the Guardian of Islam. He not only struggled under all odd conditions throughout his life with a view to teach lessons of better living, free from crimes, sins and paganism to the people but also left the comprehensive message highlighting the salient features of his mission for the posterity which would prove a mile stone in their lives and go a long way in shaping the destiny of the people. He beautifully summed up the fundamentals of Islam and reminded Muslims of their responsibilities which fell upon them in lieu of accepting Islam as a belief system. He highlighted the sanctity of human life, property and honour and forbade people to shed the blood of innocent people. He reminded human beings about their duties towards the money, wealth, property or other matters kept with them as trust and asked them to handover them to their rightful owners. He emphasized the responsibilities of the individuals and held that nobody was responsible for the act committed by an individual save himself. He forbade a Muslim from oppressing another Muslim and held that Muslims were brothers in faith but they had no ownership rights upon their properties save that which was voluntarily bestowed upon them by their brothers. He abolished all the evil practices of the age of ignorance including taking of blood revenge and he himself forgave the guilty of his clans.

Likewise, he abolished the practice of taking and giving of interest but allowed them to recover their principals and he remitted the portion of interest which was due to him. He pinpointed the rights of men and women and declared that women had rights over men and men had rights over women and asked them to honour them. He, however, permitted men to chastise their women in case of minor lapses but mildly. He told them to feed them and clothe them according to their capacities. He declared the right of inheritance to the rightful owners and ordained death by stoning to adulterers. He warned them of the dangers of Satan in matters of religion but assured them that he who followed Holy Quran and Sunna (Practices of Holy Prophet) shall never be led astray. He gave much more importance to the rights of slaves and those who work under them and asked them to feed them that which they eat and cloth them those which they wear and ignore their mistakes and not to chastise them but be kind to them. He summarized the five fundamental principles of Islam that is, faith in one true God, five times regular prayers in a day, fasting in the month of Ramadan, paying of zakat in time and performing of Hajj and obey what he said so that they might go to the heaven. He asked them to convey what he said to others and then looked at the sky proclaiming "Lord! I have conveyed your message fully. Be witness to me."

His speech indeed was a Fundamental Code of Human Rights which beautifully summed up rights of human beings for life, liberty, property, honour and justice and belief systems. He taught the lessons of universal brotherhood by emphasizing the common ancestry and common heritage of mankind and raised the status of women and the weaker sections of the society in the eyes of the civilized society. Needless to say that the rights that the Guide of Islam emphasized are found in Conventions on Civil and political Rights, Universal Declaration of Human Rights and the U.N. Declaration on the Standard Minimum Rules for the treatment of Offenders which have been ratified practically by all nations of the world.

NOTES

1. Abdul Hameed Siddiqui, op. cit., pp. 237-38.
2. *Ibid.*, 238.
3. Safiur Rahman al-Mubarakpuri, op. cit., p. 355.
4. Abdul Hameed Siddiqui, op. cit., pp. 239-40.
5. *Ibid.*, p. 240.
6. Safiur Rahman al-Mubarakpuri, op. cit., p. 354.
7. *Ibid.*, p. 359.
8. *Ibid.*
9. *Ibid.*, p. 360.
10. *Ibid.*
11. Abdul Hameed Siddiqui, op. cit., pp. 283-84.
12. Safiur Rahman al-Mubarakpuri, op. cit., p. 417.
13. Abdul Hameed Siddiqui, op. cit., p. 300.
14. *Ibid.*, p. 302.

7

The Exalted Personality and the Exemplary Conducts of the Guide of Islam

It is indeed humanly impossible to explain the exalted personality and the exemplary conducts of the Ruler of Islam who was ornamented with perfect attributes, superb character, kind heart and extra ordinary genius and who was most honoured among the people of the world. It were his exceptional qualities that brought all segments of the society closer to him and compelled them to love him, follow him and die for him. He became so popular within a short period of time that the resistance and the enmity of his adversaries started declining and people embraced his religion in multitude. Just as he was honest, trust worthy, just, compassionate, loving and merciful so also he was smart, handsome, graceful, dignified and charming. The world had never seen any Ruler as noble, as princely, alluring, pleasing and winsome as the Steward of Islam. He was not only majestic and splendid in conducts, magnanimous and magnificent in behaviour and courteous and loving in dealings but also incomparable and unique in shape, beautiful and appealing in stature and imposing and wholesome in personality.

DESCRIPTION OF THE GRAND PERSONALITY OF THE RULER

To describe his grace, grandeur and majesty is beyond the reach of every creature. Here is a brief summary of various versions about his grand personality, superb conducts and extreme perfections which earned him the titles of the most 'Handsome' the extremely 'Appealing', the highly 'Truthful', the earnestly 'Trustworthy' and 'The Mercy upon Mankind.' The brief review of his personality merely reflects a fraction of his majesty and grace and no man in the universe can ever explain what he was for save Allah no one can claim to have full knowledge about his essence and attributes.

The Ruler of Islam was such a perfect gift of God, so peerless being in shape, so gracious person in beauty, so exemplary human being in manners and so divine messenger in conducts that no one else was endowed with before. He was singularly bright, perfectly healthy and absolutely fresh. He was an exceptional man, loving leader, compassionate chief and was so dignified and glorious that he was honoured and revered by those who saw him. He was not only utterly good-looking, most handsome and highly graceful but the depth of feelings in his dark-black and large eyes with long haired eyelids, finely arched by continuous and naturally groomed eyebrows mesmerized the onlookers beyond imagination. His beautiful eyebrows were not joined and had a vein between them that glowed in case of anger. His delightful and slightly spacious and elegant broad-round face not only glittered like the full moon but the winning smile and a pleasant expression on his splendid countenance attracted people at first sight. By his fair-pink colour, wide-broad forehead and a charming smile on his glamorous lips, he won each heart. He had moustaches and His high-tipped straight and middle-cambered nose with narrow nostrils having special glow had an extreme type of attraction for everyone who came in his contact.[1] When he graciously addressed someone, mysterious light passed through a small space between his two front teeth. When he was in happy mood, he magnificently laughed but his laughter was limited to the extent of his sweet smile. His moderately built body and very strong and powerful stature provided grace and elegance to his pleasing personality. His finely proportionate and admirable body which was neither fat nor thin nor bulging made him unique among his companions. Since his belly and the chest were in the same level, he looked very agile and smart. Likewise, his broad shoulders, wide and smooth chest, long forearms, big limbs and a little above average or medium height neither too high nor too small and stately and majestic form was brilliant and dignified. His well formed, large and towering head set on a slender, silvery and doll-like neck provided him extraordinary dignity and charm. His long, glossy black hair both wavy and inclined to curve that is neither curly nor straight added to his beauty and grandeur. His hair which went up to his earlobes look graceful and his few scattered grey hairs in his head and thick beard glittered like gems and jewels.[2] His chest without hair was alluring and the hair on his arms and shoulders looked wonderful. Likewise, his hair from the end of his breastbone to his navel were highly praiseworthy. With his firm body joints, large forearms, wide palms and moderately lengthy fingers and splendid hands and feet he looked rarest of the rare.

When he was sitting his unfolded hands, well-shaped but cool, soft, silky and thick and expansive hand palms and thick fingers and fine toes and lean heels fascinated everyone. When he moved his gentle, delicate, plain and straight legs remained in conformity and they stretched down and the two hollows of his soles hardly touched the ground. He walked in strides and in a graceful manner. While walking he leant forward, lifted his feet off the ground and walked at ease and did not drag them.[3] His walk conveyed strength and resolution. He moved softly and firmly with large swift strides. His Companions found it hard to keep pace with him even though he walked leisurely. It looked as if the ground appeared to roll itself up to him. When he turned, he turned fully. When he pointed at any object he would do so with his full-hand-palm and when he showed any surprise he would turn it round. His body smelt like musk and ambergris. His sweat was scented and pear-like and when he passed through any route people could know from his body smell that the Messenger of God had passed through that way. The Seal of Prophethood which was equal to a pigeon's egg was between his shoulders on the left side having spots on it like moles.

HIS GRACIOUS MANNERS

His voice was melodious, sweet and extremely charming and commanding. His expression was distinct, contemplative, serene and sublime. He spoke clearly and uttered meaningful, precise and accurate statements only. His utterances were highly decisive and no one could distort them. His speech was well set and finely connected like the rosary of beads and free from superfluous words. His sermons were very appealing and convincing, meaningful and thought-provoking. He was a reliable, accurate and unpretending straightforward speaker. He was renowned for his superb eloquence, fluency in arabic and spoke with his entertainers in their own dialects and accents. He had mastered and was eloquent both at the Bedouin language and the clarity and the decorated splendor of the town speech. He would normally remain silent for a long time and spoke when it was necessary and closely relevant to him. Whatever, he said was inclusive, meaningful, amiable, clear and final. It was not too excessive nor too short of meaning. He asked his people to do what was right and invited others towards it and forbade what was wrong and stopped others from doing that. He confirmed what was right and permissible and undermined that which was awful and non-permissible. When he finished his speech, he did it gracefully by glorifying the bounty of the Lord. He never forgot to remember the Lord while sitting or standing and asked others to do the same.

The Steward of Islam remained in thoughtful mood for most of the time. He was a good listener and keenest and most attentive to people's worries, problems and grievances. He was most careful of people's trust and was renowned for his trustworthiness. When he was pleased his face would shine with so much light that it appeared as if the sun-light was moving on his face and it was then that his teeth which were like white pearls were revealed. When he was angry or displeased his face would go red and he would turn both his body and face aside. Whoever saw him was fascinated from a distance but when he became familiar, he was enchanted and overwhelmed with bliss in his heart and never forgot him till he died. He was ready to sacrifice his life, persons and possessions willingly even to save a scratch on Holy Ruler's body. The Guardian of Islamic state was genius, far-sighted, gifted and wise to the fullest extent of his mental capacity. No man on earth had intellect as perfect, complete, sound and excellent as he. Those who read his unique biography, examined his pious conducts, pondered over his state of affairs, analyzed his meaningful and lofty utterances, learnt about the systems and traditions left by him were amazed that how could an 'Un-lettered personality' who had no formal schooling and who neither read the old scriptures nor sat with their scholars could have excellent knowledge of Torah, Gospel and other divine scriptures as well as the knowledge of bygone nations? How could he have the perfection in the art of statecraft, extreme insight of medicine, fine knowledge of jurisprudence, insight of science, niceties of arts and intricacies of worship, morality, spiritualism and what not? He was able to provide wisdom to people, guide them on the right path and teach them the mysteries of the world and the hereafter only because he was bestowed by the Lord by the knowledge of all such things.

He was the embodiment of exceptional virtues and his hospitality, generosity, stamina, endurance, patience and forgiveness were fathomless. He would meet everybody with such a welcoming and cheerful mood that he would think that he was the most beloved of all to him. Whomever he met righteousness was his ornament and he wore the robe of piousness and was neither lacking in it nor was indifferent to it. The more he was hurt or injured, the more he became patient and the more insolence was exercised upon him, the more enduring he became. Whenever he got the opportunity to chose between the two permissible and good alternatives he chose the one that was easiest and the most convenient. He lived for Allah's cause and not for himself. He never took a personal revenge and he was the first to be satisfied and last to get angry. Once Holy Prophet went on an expedition along with his companions and on their way back they rested in a valley under the shades of trees. The Prophet hung his sword on a branch, spread out his cloak and slept. A Bedouin who was following them came quietly and took the sword in his hands and cried. "O Muhammad! Who is going to protect you from me now?" When Holy Prophet woke up he found that the Bedouin had his sword in his hands and he was bent upon killing him. He minded the least though he was alone. When the Bedouin repeatedly shouted, "Who would save you now?" The Holy Prophet replied with full confidence and conviction, "Allah". The Bedouin was terror struck and the sword fell from his hands. Holy Prophet took hold of the sword and told him, "Who would save you from me now?" The Bedouin got frightened and fell on his feet and begged mercy The Holy Prophet forgave him without any hesitation.[4] He never feared poverty and generously showered gifts and endowments upon the needy and the helpless. He never denied anything he was asked for. One day a woman out of love gave a beautiful woolen gown to Holy Prophet which she had woven by her hands. He relished it most but when a Companion requested for it he gave it immediately.[5] He was innocent as a child, compassionate as a father, affectionate as a husband, helping as a neighbour, honest as a merchant, sincere as a preacher, considerate as an emigrant, reliable as a friend, brave as a warrior, proactive as a commander, forgiving as a conqueror, just as a judge, sympathetic as a ruler, genius as a law-giver, exceptional as a human being and above all a devoted servant to Almighty God. He was gifted with a kind heart, brilliant brain, depthless insight, sublime thoughts, unmatchable intuition, superb imagination and delicacy of feelings.

He was extremely brave, highly courageous and most dauntless. He witnessed awkward and heart-breaking times but stood fast at them. More than once he was left alone in the thick and the thin of battle surrounded by dreaded enemies but he stood with full confidence, composure and courage facing them alone without turning his back. He always fought in the front and being closest to enemies provided succor to his colleagues during difficult times. Very often when he smelt any danger to the town he went alone with sword hanging around his neck to verify it on horseback which had no saddle. He was highly modest and shier than the veiled virgin.[6] He glanced his eyes modestly at people who had their eyes casted down due to solemnity and never stared at anybody's face and was the first one to cast his eyes down. He generally looked at the ground more than he looked upward. He hated the crime and not the criminals. When an alcoholic person was brought before the ruler of Islam in drunken state, it was decreed that he be lashed. A few days later he was again spotted drunk and he was brought before the ruler and he was lashed.

A few days later he was again found drinking and brought in Ruler's presence, he was lashed. After pronouncing the punishment when the Ruler was leaving, he heard a Companion saying, "May Allah curse him! How often he has come here to be lashed! The Compassionate Ruler turned to him and told him, 'Do not curse him.' By Allah! I know that he loves Allah and His Messenger."[7] He never called a person by name and did not name a person about whom he had heard some adverse comments and never cursed even his dreaded enemies but prayed the Lord to give them guidance. He did not swear at anyone nor humiliated him. When he did not like the act of any individual he would say: "What is wrong with him, may dust be cast in his face."[8] When he was hurt, harmed and abused by people he never made noise in the street but calmly and quietly tolerated everything. He never avenged himself but became angry only when people transgressed the limits set by Allah. If he disliked anything one could sense it from his facial expressions. He never replied offence by offence but pushed back the offence and error by forgiveness and overlooking. He never uttered even "Uf" or "Ugh" before the servants and never rebuked or blamed them for not doing anything or doing something wrong. Anas said that he worked with the Merciful Ruler of Islam for nine years but "I never heard him comment about anything I did, 'Why did you do this?' He never criticized me for anything at all. By Allah! He never even said uf to me."[9] Likewise, in one night when Kulthum bin al-Husayb was with him in the valley of Al-Akhdar during the Tabuk expedition his camel's saddle brushed against the Ruler's foot while he was in sleep. He woke up from sleep hearing the sigh of the Hoy Ruler. He was embarrassed seeing him in utter pain and begged his forgiveness upon which the Kind Ruler demonstrated extreme tolerance and replied "Carry on. Carry on."[10] He was sincere and honest in all his matters and never believed in reprimanding, disparaging, or reproaching people. Likewise, he neither found the faults of the people nor looked at their weaknesses, defects and shortcomings. If he noticed some person making the mistake, he would not confront him directly but would generalize it by saying, "What is with the people, who do such and such?" He was never partial in delivering justice but pronounced his judgments truthfully. The extremely Just Ruler of Islam decreed in one case that her hand be cut off. Since the woman belonged to a respectable family of Quraish the reputed people deputed Usamah bin Zayd the most beloved person to the Exalted Ruler of Islam with a view to lighten the punishment. When Usamah pleaded for the woman, he got angry and told people around him. "The people before you were only destroyed because when a noble person from amongst them stole, they left him, and when a weak person stole, they implemented the legal punishment on him. I swear by the One who has my soul in His Hand, if Fatimah the daughter of Muhammad were to steal, I would cut off her hand."[11] It was because of his proper execution of justice that during his times the law and order position was so excellent that a woman laden with gold could be able to travel alone without any male guardian or without any protection from Al-Hira to Makkah.

He loved the children, played with them and cut jokes with them. Holy Prophet used to play with the brother of Anas bin Malik and had nicknamed him Abu' Umayr. The child had a small bird that he played with. Whenever the Holy Prophet would meet him he would joke with him saying, "O Abu' Umayr, what happened to al-Nughayr?" meaning the bird.[12] Similarly, one day Umm Qays bint Muhsin came to the Ruler of Islam with her new born child to get his blessings while he was sitting. He took the child and placed him in his lap. The child urinated and made his garment wet. He showed no reaction but asked for some water, spread over the affected area of the garment and that was the end of the matter."[13] He entertained even illiterate Bedouins and mentally derailed people. Once he was wearing a Yemeni cloak with a collar with rough edges. A Bedouin grabbed him strongly and sought his help. Though the edges of the cloak had left marks on his neck, he did not mind but smiled and ordered to pay him some money.[14] Likewise, a woman from Medina who was partially insane stopped him and told him that she was in trouble. He not only helped her but also looked after her problems.[15] He entertained the poor and did not hesitate in getting intimate with them.

A Bedouin named Zahir b. Hram used to give gifts to Holy Prophet and prepare things for him. Once he came to meet the Prophet but did not find him and left for the market. When the Splendid Ruler of Islam came to know of him he went to the market where he was selling his goods and hugged him from behind. He could not see him and said leave me. When he came to know of the Holy Prophet he pressed his back towards the Messenger's chest and the Messenger of God entertained him despite the fact that his look was not very appealing and he was not wearing clean and nice clothes.[16] He was not only kind to the human beings but also loved the birds and animals. When he found the bird flapping its wings, the Holy Prophet asked his companions who had disturbed the bird? When he came to know that someone had taken its two chicks he asked him to return the same immediately.[17] Likewise, on another occasion when he observed the nest of the ants burnt. He asked who did it? He got very angry upon his companion who had done that and forbade them never do it again in future.[18] Similarly, when he observed two persons conversing while saddling on the backs of the sitting camels he told them to show mercy towards them and not to use camels as their chairs.[19] He attended the sick irrespective of the fact whether they were Muslims or not. Once he went to see the Jewish child who was seriously ill and remained there till he died. Similarly, he participated in the funerals of the people and showed regards for the dead of all communities. Once when the dead body of a Jew was being carried, he stood up as a mark of respect towards the dead. He never showed any contempt towards the have-nots or never belittled or disgraced any person due to poverty, ignorance, disease or any handicap. He hated lying and if anyone lied before him he would catch hold of him and did not leave him till he repented.[20] Similarly, he abhorred the persecution and when someone was harmed, he would not sit quiet till justice was done to him. He hated to be privileged and participated in all the tasks along with his companions. Even his hardened enemies acknowledged his noble and sterling qualities and during the days of ignorance they used to come to him for consultations and judgment.

UPRIGHT RULER

Unlike his contemporary kings and Emperors he was most simple, modest and humble and too far from being called an arrogant or proud. When he entered Makkah as a triumphant Ruler, he was highly polite and humble. During this time a man came and asked some questions but his hands were shivering out of fear. The Holy Ruler told him to take it easy as he was merely the son of a woman from Quraish who used to eat dried meat. He forbade people to stand up at his presence as had been the practice since unknown times. One day a delegation from Al-Sadif consisting of ten people came to the Ruler of Islam and they sat among the gathering without giving salutation. After confirming from them that they were Muslims, he asked them why did they not give salutation? They stood up to give the reply but he told them, "Please be seated."[21] He never allowed anyone to walk behind him as his bodyguard. No specific position was assigned for him. He could sit wherever he desired among people. He would usually sit at the end of the group or next to the last sitter and advised others not to crossover people but sit as he did. He treated himself as equal to others and never considered him as one elevated and superior to others. In his opinion no one was better than others due to wealth, family background, colour, place of birth and any worldly distinction. He never felt superior compared even to the slaves in matters of food and clothing. For him the best of all and the distinguished in ranks were those who helped him in Allah's cause and provided consultations, succor and comforts to him. He entertained all people alike while sitting in any social gathering and never gave the impression that such and such was great or the privileged one. The one who sat next to him and interrupted him with a view to ask for some advice about any of his personal affairs was generally the first to start the talk and the one to end it. The person considered himself the most privileged one as being the first to be heard. Holy Prophet listened him patiently till he finished his speech and replied him to his entire satisfaction. The Islamic Ruler was always surrounded by his companions and whatever he uttered the listeners would hear him with rapt attention and whenever he issued any command they vied with each other in carrying it out. When he spoke there was pin drop silence and his listeners listened him casting their heads down. They would spoke only when he was silent. There was no dispute in matters of who would speak first for he who talked in his presence was heard well attentively till he finished his speech. Others too talked about the topics discussed earlier or the one delivered by the first speaker. He was mostly silent. However, if he found someone speaking inoffensive or unbecoming tone, he turned away from those whose speech was rude and impolite. He would never deny a request made by anyone and tried to satisfy by uttering few gratifying words. Because of his large-hearted tolerance, magnanimity, broad-mindedness and love for all he was a fatherly figure for all. The Guardian of Islam had produced commendable people around him. They were essentially right-minded people who possessed great respects for the old and showered mercy upon their young. They were the people who never raised voices in rows or created riot like situations and believed in honesty, patience and clemency and never made inviolable things violable and fearing Allah they sought consolation in worship, adoration and the betterment of mankind.

HIS HUMAN RELATIONS

The gracious Ruler cared for human relations to his utmost. He was always lenient and met people cheerfully, smilingly, pleasantly and informally. He was never rude, rough, indecent, clamorous or discourteous. He never believed in reproaching or praising people but ignored or overlooked things he did not like. He despised hypocrisy, superfluous things and unnecessary indulgence in matters which did not concern him. He had full control over his temper and never showed any anger unless and until it was necessary for the cause of Allah. He accepted the invitation if a slave invited him and made it a point to visit those who invited him. If he had not liked any food he neither praised it nor criticized it. He was always found sitting among his friends and companion as if he was one of them. Ill-manners and indecency were alien to him. He developed the relationship of brotherhood among his companions, made them intimate and never separated them from him. Those who were honourable, dignified and chiefs among the tribes, he gave them respect and honour and bestowed upon them high positions and made them rulers upon their own people. He provided cheerfulness upon every face and everyone felt most comfortable and at ease in his august company. He never took things lightly and tackled each and every situation in its proper perspective.

HE LIKED GOOD THINGS AND WAS ATTACHED TO HIS FAMILY

It would not be out of place to mention here that the Exalted Ruler did not abandon the use of good things in life. He liked the tasty food, relished the beauty of the flowers, enjoyed the fragrance of the perfumes and indulged in light jokes. He had special affection about the little children. He used to stop them in the street and patted their heads with love and compassion. In leisure times, he did not hesitate to participate in their innocent games. He admired the excellent qualities of others and readily accepted the sound council no matter from whichever source it came. He was a warmhearted and trustworthy friend. He was highly attached to his kith and kin and intimately affectionate to his family. He loved the members of his family, friends, companions and the strangers affectionately. He immensely loved all his wives and had fathomless love for his daughter Fatimah and her husband Ali and cherished Al-Hasan and Al-Husayn, the sons of his daughter more than his life. It happened many times that they sat on his back while their grandfather was in prostration during his prayers and he did not raise his head until they came down. One day during Dhuhr or Asr prayer he stayed longer than usual such that the companion thought that either something had happened or he was receiving revelation. On asking, "the Ruler of Islamic Kingdom replied that his son was riding on his back and he did not think it proper to take off so quickly until he had finished."[22] He had a deep love, affection and regard for his old friend Abu Bakr and treated him like his brother. Likewise, he cherished Ali, his cousin and son-in-law as well as Zayd, a freed slave like his sons. He had a great affinity and intense liking for Umar and Uthman and acknowledged with deep sense of appreciation the timely help given by Ansar in the cause of Islam. He was very kind, obliging and helpful to everyone. With the exception of one who opened an open challenge to him, he never reacted. He never asked questions like who has come to him or why has he come at such an odd time but welcomed each and everybody with open heart. While shaking hands he was extremely courteous and never withdrew his hand out of another man's palm till the other one loosed it and did not turn away before the other one turned away.

THE DAILY ROUTINE OF THE RULER OF ISLAM

The daily routine of the Guardian of Islam was very rigorous and meaningful. He got up early in the morning and after his morning prayers taught wisdom to people, purified their hearts and educated his followers in principles and practices of Islam and the niceties of the Islamic jurisprudence. He received envoys and foreign dignitaries and discussed with them the national and international matters and dictated dispatches. After this he met the local people heard their grievances settled their disputes and administered justice. Finally, the assembly was dissolved. After the public function was over he used to go to one of his Empresses and helped her in doing any job she wanted him to do. He even went on shopping in the market to bring household material needed in the house. Likewise, after another short prayer he visited the sick, infirm, weak and poor and asked them their problems and helped them accordingly. A weak and lean slave girl often met him and complained about the arrogance, excesses and exploitation of her master. He would set out with her to see her owner and to mediate on her behalf.[23] Having done this, he made it a point to call his friends at their houses and pass time in their sweet company while discussing vital matters of religion and the state. After that he went to the mosque for noon-day prayer and from there returned to the home and took meal if it was available and then retired to his private apartment for rest and then again moved to the mosque for afternoon prayers. After the prayers he visited his empresses and passed his time in their company and played and enjoyed with children till the evening time arrived. As soon as he heard the Adhan for evening prayer, he moved to the mosque, finished the prayers and took his supper and did his household affairs or spent his time in teaching Islam to his followers. Finally, he led the night prayers in the mosque and came to his home for some rest. He slept for a while and then got up and prayed and meditated and again retired and slept for a while and got up as usual in early morning for morning prayers. It is highly astonishing to note that while doing all the vigorous work mentioned above he never fatigued but was always found fresh and smiling.

We have read the biographies of most famous men in history some of whom raised powerful armies, established mighty empires, gave law codes and administered people rationally, compassionately and justly and earned the titles of the conquerors of the world. A few were called greatest because of their courage, conviction, bravery, genius and farsightedness and there were many who did not frame legislations, moved armies, established dynasties but discovered virgin lands, mighty continents and were honoured by kings and emperors. There were several scientists who did not affect people, societies, customs and conventions but made discoveries and inventions and revolutionized the theoretical concepts and prevailing systems for which they were awarded noble and distinguished prizes and there was no dearth of people who gave the world new belief systems, taught them the lessons of piety and righteousness for which they were adored with reverence and placed in the temples, churches and monasteries. As against this, the world has never seen a person who was born and brought up in odd conditions, did not inherit any land, title or property but was helpless and support less and was persecuted, boycotted and deserted merely for telling the truth and bringing people from ignorance to light. The same man in the capacity of the Last Prophet of God and the Ruler of Islamic State, not only moved armies, empires, dynasties, kingdoms, nations, countries and people but revolutionized religions, belief systems, ideas and ideologies and concepts. He conquered hearts, minds and souls of the people for all times to come and guided them, purified their consciences and made their conducts exemplary. He provided them peace, prosperity and contentment in this world and opened the gates for salvation, bliss and meaningful and purposeful life in the Hereafter. If we turn the pages of history we do not find any person of his eminence who single-handed did what all the greatest men of the world could not do in unison. The Ruler of Islam possessed miracles and divine powers but he did not use them. Instead, he did wonderful things by his extraordinary behaviour and never boasted for any of his achievements and forcefully disclaimed divinity for himself. Such a majestic Ruler, judged by all standards of greatness and magnanimity can be placed without any shred of doubt on such a loftiest heights of exaltedness which was never achieved by any man on earth.

THE TRAITS OF ANCIENT EMPERORS AND MONARCHS

Many important Universities, institutes, centers and academies were established in the United States of America, Europe, Australia, South America, Africa and Asia to impart teaching in the field of good governance, politics, war strategies, leadership, public administration, financial management and human relations but the outcome turned out to be quite contrary to what was expected. The ancient Kings, Emperors, Rulers and Monarchs were mainly interested in the safety, security of their kingdoms and the luxurious patterns of their lives rather than the betterment of the people. Those reformers, thinkers, philosophers and intellectuals who rose in support of people also confined their approach merely to material development rather than the holistic development of human personality. Consequently, the Emperors, Monarchs, Kings, Dictators, Nobles, Chiefs, Leaders and Rulers instead of becoming their saviours, guides and friends became their masters. They exploited them by their might and there was none to challenge them. Their hunger for power, prestige, name and fame prompted them to win territories, subjugate people, usurp people's resources and shed the blood of innocent men, women, aged, sick and the handicapped. Their visions, missions and strategies were confined merely to the extent of proving their superiority, grandeur and magnanimity over others. Some of them moved with their mighty infantries from Central Asia and destroyed the forts, fortresses, castles, mansions and reached as far as India. Others turned towards Middle East equipped with their strong cavalries and erected the towers of victories from the severed heads of the vanquished people in Babul, Jerusalem and Egypt. There was no dearth of the ambitious generals who turned towards China and ruined the fields, orchards, bazaars, huts, hamlets and pillars of ancient civilizations merely to show their might and superiority. Many Monarchs like the Pharaohs of Egypt declared themselves as gods, several kings considered themselves as the progenies of sun and moon gods and there were a few fortunate ones whose statutes were worshipped in temples, monasteries and religious places as real gods. Kings were supposed to do no wrong since they were immune from the laws of the land. They could usurp any property, humiliate or kill any man, make any woman concubine and destroy the crops, orchards and fields of the people for their pleasure and pass time. They could not afford to hear no or any dissent and defiance. Those who dared to raise any voice against them were brutally killed, tortured or banished from their lands. Providing peace, prosperity and building the social and cultural institution on sound lines, leading the people on the path of righteousness and making their conducts exemplary did not fall within their domains.

The mighty forts and strong fortresses well protected and amply fortified and magnificent palaces and mansions decorated with gems and jewels fancied them. Most of them enjoyed the company of the nobles, courtiers, consultants and the advisors. They passed their time in enjoying horse riding, arrow shooting, sword practicing and hunting. Very often they moved with their paraphernalia for sightseeing, picnic parties and outings. Self praise, flattery and acts of their braveries, large-hearted tolerance and magnificence pleased them. They did not tolerate defiance, insubordination and stubbornness. Whoever rebelled or mutinied or rose against them was wiped out of the face of their kingdoms. They did not hesitate in mounting attacks upon their adversaries, destroying the powers of their enemies and shedding the blood of their foes. Many of them enjoyed the bloody games, dual fights between the furious lions and men. They relished tasty foods of various kinds, wore wonderful robes studded with costly diamonds and decorated their bodies with rarest ornaments. Their crowns were unmatchable, their thrones were unrivalled and their darbars were unparalleled.

THE APPROACH OF THE RULER OF ISLAM

As against this, the gracious steward of Islam was a remarkable Ruler, reformer, guide and friend. His impact upon humanity and his mercy upon mankind are so obvious that he shall always be remembered as the savior of mankind. His canvas covered the political and secular as well as religious and spiritual activities of his people. He thought of the worldly benefits of his subjects as well as prepared them for the better hereafter. He inspired firm belief in the hearts of the people about one true God, taught them the art of worship and adoration, told them to pay charity, taught them civilized manners, improved their socio-economic conditions and made them good human beings. His uniqueness lies in the fact that he completely revolutionized the everyday life of human beings and changed the lifestyle of the people which was not much different from what it was between 1600 B.C. and 600 A.D. It was he who taught the lessons of universal brotherhood by emphasizing that all mankind came from Adam and Adam was created from dust. He was the pioneer and the champion of Human Rights and prior to him nobody could think that all people were equal in all respects and an Arab was not superior to non-Arab so also a red-faced was not better than the black one except in piety. He said that shedding the blood of one another and usurping of one another's property was unlawful and likewise, he held that it was unlawful to violate the honours of human beings. He advised people to maintain cordial relations with human beings and provide food and extend greetings to one whom they knew or knew not. He invited the attention of the people towards charity by saying that to remove something harmful from the road was charity.

Charity, in his opinion, erased the sins as water extinguished fire. He forcefully told that none amongst them was a true believer till he liked for his brother that which he loved for himself. He repeated several times that he would not enter paradise whose neighbours were not secure from his mischievous conducts. He also reminded people that he was not a perfect believer who went to bed full of stomach and knew that his neighbour was hungry. He compared the believers with human body and said that if the eye was in agony, the entire body felt the pain and when the head ached, the whole body would suffer. Similarly, if one believer was in trouble the whole set of believers suffered equally. He also exhorted people to show mercy to human beings on earth so that the Lord may show His mercy upon them in the heaven. He guided people to treat women equitably showing utmost regards for them. He went to the extent of saying that the heaven was beneath the feet of mothers. He asked people to respect the elders and love the younger and be good to all. He warned the people not to indulge in drinking, gambling, backbiting and lewd activities. In a sense he provided a complete code of conduct for the people to live better life in this world as well as to get salvation after death. The world has not produced any ruler, thinker or leader till date who could think so seriously about the multi-dimensional aspects of the entire humanity save the guide of Islam.

His greatest contribution in the war and the world strategies is that he provided a dynamic, fruitful and most effective strategy of faith in God to his followers to confront worldly and divine problems. Neither he gave his warriors the innovative means to fight war nor he relied on weapons, warriors and wealth to fight the enemy but he fought with faith in God with the conviction that since he was on the right path his victory was destined. Many generals in stone age succeeded in conquering their enemies fighting with stones as they had invented arrows, some commanders enslaved the hunters with the might of the discovery of agriculture, a few routed the enemies fighting on foot since they were riding on the horse backs, several ruled the people with the power of their cannons, a select few routed their sword-fighting foes due to the superiority of their guns. The allies routed axis powers merely on the strength of their atom bombs.

The Ruler of Islam did nothing of this sort. For thirteen years he taught his companions in Makkah that there was only One Unique and the Supreme God who was the creator, nurturer and the destroyer of the created world. It was He to whom belonged the heavens and the earth, kingdoms and the territories. It was the Lord who provided victories and defeats. It was He who guided people by sending his messengers in the world with scriptures and guidance to lead them on straight path. Thus, he who wanted victory and success on the battle field or in the world, it was incumbent upon him that he should firmly believe in His Lord and fight against the wicked and the perpetuators of sins and crimes with the strategy of faith which was bound to lead him on the path of success. When he succeeded in establishing an Islamic state at Medina, he applied his strategy of faith on war fronts and in worldly affairs with the result that he routed his mighty enemies despite his weak position.

NOTES

1. Abdurrahman al-Sheha, op. cit., p. 23.
2. *Ibid.*
3. *Ibid.*, p. 24.
4. Dr. Muhammad Al-Afreefi, op. cit., p. 84.
5. Abdurrahman al-Sheha, op. cit., p. 34.
6. Al-Bukhari, 5751.

7. *Ibid.*, 6780.
8. *Ibid.*, 5684.
9. Dr. Muhammad Al-Afreefi, op. cit., p. 211.
10. *Ibid.*, p. 296.
11. *Ibid.*, p. 265.
12. *Ibid.*, p. 75.
13. *Ibid.*, p. 299.
14. Abdurrahman al-Sheha, op. cit., p. 42.
15. *Ibid.*, p. 41.
16. *Ibid.*, p. 52.
17. Dr. Muhammad Al-Afreefi, op. cit., p. 91.
18. *Ibid.*
19. *Ibid.*, p. 90.
20. Tirmidthi, 1973.
21. Dr. Muhammad Al-Afreefi, pp. 284-85.
22. *Ibid.*, pp. 297-98.
23. *Ibid.*, p. 438.

8

The Possessions and Personal Life of the Ruler of Islam

If we now look at his palaces and forts and fortresses we find that he had none. He executed all his policies from the courtyard of the mosque. When he reached Medina in 622 A.D., the first thing that he did was to construct a mosque. A suitable and ideal site was selected and purchased from the two orphans after paying them ten gold coins and then the land was donated for the construction of the mosque. The land was cleared of weeds, shrubs, palm trees and rubbish. The mosque was fifty yards long and fifty yards wide and faced towards the north with three gates in the remaining three sides. The northern door was meant for the entrance of general public, the western gate was called Bab al-Rahman and the eastern gate was reserved for Prophet's household called 'Bab al-Nisa.' Adjoining the mosque were constructed two apartments for the family of the Head of Islamic kingdom. To the north of the mosque was a seminary attached to the mosque. There lived 'Ashab al-Suffah' or the people of the Sufah who had no homes and no families but had devoted their whole lives for the study of the religion. The mosque was a monument of simplicity. Its walls were constructed of mud and bricks and the roof was supported by the trunks of the palm trees. Since the roof was covered by palm leaves and twigs it could not stop the rain water which many a time made the unpaved floor muddy.

THE PALACES AND THE FORTS OF THE RULER

The Exalted Chief of Islam's apartments were extremely simple even simpler than the mosque. They were built of stones and adobe bricks with ceiling of palm trees. Some rooms were built of raw bricks whereas others were mere cells made up of twigs and palm trees. To provide privacy and seclusion to the inmates of the family, worn out blankets were used on the doors and entry points. During the caliphate of Uthman when people visited the Empresses of the Ruler of Islamic Kingdom, they found the ceilings so low that they could be touched by hands. Dawud bin Qays said that he had the good fortune to see with his own eyes the quarters where the Empresses of His majesty the Holy Prophet resided. These were apartments made out of the branches of palm trees, and blankets of camel-hair hung at their doors. The courtyard was hardly six to seven paces in length and breadth and rooms did not extend beyond ten paces. After the death of the Empresses all the quarters were annexed to the mosque for extension purposes. Were these rooms kept intact, the world would have seen the simple and austere living of the Islamic Ruler?[1]

If we now look at the mansions, palaces and forts and fortresses of Kings, Emperors and Monarchs of the world we find that they were the monuments of glamour, beauty and majesty. Their mammoth sizes, imposing heights, strong structures, heavy fortifications impressed the friends and deterred the enemies. Likewise, the charms of their magnificent mansions, beauty of their spacious lawns, splendor of their beautiful gardens, agility of their alert watchmen and the patterns of their colorful flags fascinated each and everyone. Despite all these the grace, dignity and reverence that was there in the apartments of the Ruler of Islam built of stones and adobe bricks were far better than the grandeur, grace and glory of all the palaces of the Kings, Monarchs and Emperors of the world. Similarly, the magnificence, majesty and pomp and show which is there in the Presidential palaces can hardly match with the noble, sublime and pious structure of the Ruler of Islam. Every spot of his pious house is the symbol of Islam's dignity, every inch of it is more than the value of all the wealth of the created world and every centimeter of it commands that love and affection which the glorious and the mightiest Mansions of the greatest people of the world do not command.

After having gone through the simplicity of the lifestyle of the Exalted Ruler one would surely be convinced that the Steward of Islam was certainly a different kind of Ruler. Despite being the Mighty Controller of the Arabian Peninsula he conducted the functions of his Islamic state from the mudded floor of the mosque. It was in this simple and pious mosque that the ambassadors, envoys and representatives of various Kings, Emperors and Monarchs were received and entertained. It was from this mudded building that his edicts were issued to the Rulers of Persia, Egypt, Byzantines, Abyssinia, Yemen, Bahrain and others. It was the mosque where his companions met and discussed state affairs and advised the Ruler in the matters of governance. Historical records testify that the Exalted Ruler of Islamic Kingdom lived without his gorgeous and glamorous throne but this is also a fact of history that the gracious place that he occupied to govern his kingdom was far more adorable, reverent and dignified than the 17th century Peacock Throne of Mughal Shāh Jahān which was decorated with crosses of rubies and emeralds, and also with diamonds and pearls. In all there were 108 large rubies and 116 emeralds costing as per contemporary estimates value varied between ₹ 40 million and ₹ 100 million. Likewise, the Naderi gemmed and jeweled Throne of Iran too could not match the importance, significance and the piety of the mudded floor of the Mosque though it was made of wood, covered with gold, and encrusted with 26,733 jewels covering the throne including four very large spinels and four very large emeralds on the backrest, the largest of them varying between 65 carets and 225 carets. Nobody talks of the 250 year old 18th century Marble Throne of Iran consisting of 65 marble stone pieces brought from a mine in Yazd and throne's supports carved in the shape of men, women, ferries and demons. Similarly, people have forgotten the Dragon Throne of China which was made up of "white marble and jade", liberally sculptured according to the canons of Chinese art. In the same way, we do not hear about the Takht-i-Jahangiri which was made of black onyx, imported by Jahangir from Belgium. As against this, the place which the Exalted Ruler of Islam occupied for the purposes of governing the Islamic Kingdom is as important and significant today as it was fourteen hundred years ago. Millions of people across the world not only respect, adore and venerate it but also pay homage and make it a point to kiss it with extreme love, awe and reverence.

DRESS OF THE EXALTED HIGHNESS

The world knows that Kings, Emperors and Monarchs were known for their beautiful and costly dresses. Their diamond-studded robes, pearled-ornamented necklaces, gems and jewels decorated rings, sapphire and emerald patched shoes, gold-ornamented adornments were the centre of attraction for the onlookers. However, if one looks at the dresses of the Merciful Ruler of Islam one would be disheartened to see that his dress was most simple. It generally consisted of a shirt, tahmad (trousers), a sheet thrown round the shoulders and a turban. He rarely put on costly robes presented to him by foreign emissaries in the later part of his life. His blanket too was not new and costly but the old one which had several patches. He did not have so many spare clothes, but whatever little clothes he had, he kept them spotlessly clean. He wanted others also to put on simple but clean clothes. He was often found wearing a cloak, a rough garment and a thick mantle. It is claimed that when he died he had a patched garment and a thick lower garment. The above incidents indicate the modesty and humility of his dress because being proud due to beautiful clothing and adornment was not the part and parcel of his traits. Although he would wear simple and humble clothes, he paid much attention to its cleanliness, good appearance, and a nice scent. He would certainly wear beautiful clothes for the *jumu'ah* (Friday prayer) and the two 'Eids. He used to have special robe which he would wear when receiving envoys. He would give great consideration to his appearance and smell, and would love perfume. He wore dresses befitting ceremonies and occasions and advised Muslims to care for their appearances and cleanliness.[2]

HIS CROWN

Incidentally the Mighty Ruler of Islamic State did not have any crown save his simple turban which he wore during his daily routines. It was indeed more dignified, more graceful and more imposing than the Imperial State Crown of United Kingdom possessing many precious gems and jewels including 2,868 diamonds, 273 pearls, 17 sapphires, 11 emeralds, and 5 rubies. When he wore his glorious turban every crown looked before it insignificant, trivial and inconsequential including the platinum crown of Queen Elizabeth which was decorated with emeralds, rubies, sapphires, 6,100 diamonds and several precious stones, most notably the 105 carat (21 g) Koh-i-Noor diamond in the middle of the front cross. Likewise, when he came out of his house with white head geared on his majestic, splendid and magnificent head it appeared more appealing, more attractive and more fascinating than the Great Imperial Crown of Russia decorated with one of the seven historic stones of Russian diamond collections which the Emperors of Russia adorned with a row of 37 very fine large white pearls, a large precious red spinal weighing 398.72 carats and 4936 diamonds arranged in splendid patterns across the entire surface of the crown. In the same way, when he wrapped any piece of clothe around his noble, gracious and imposing head it looked better than the Imperial Crown of Holy Roman Empire made out of a high carat gold studded with 144 green and blue precious stones, pearls, sapphires, emeralds and amethysts as well as small pearls, many only 7 millimeters in diameter, stitched onto it. Even when he was without any head gear his attractive long, black and curly hair shined brighter than the 3,380 diamonds and 369 natural white pearls and 5 sizable emeralds of the Pahlavi crown made up of gold, silver and red velvet. The world does not know anything about the crowns of the mighty and the greatest rulers. Several of them have been looted, many of them have been destroyed with time and a few of them are lying unclaimed and unattended in the museums. As compared to this his outstanding, eventful and momentous turban is the symbol of Islam's elegance, simplicity and piety.

THE RETINUE AND THE SUPPORTING STAFF OF THE HEAD OF THE STATES

Buckingham Palace is an official place for the Head of State, as well as a home for The Queen. As of now over 800 working hands are based at Buckingham Palace. Their jobs range from housekeeping to horticulture, catering to correspondence. Some of the more unusual jobs include fendersmith, clockmaker and flagman. Similarly there are several palaces of the Kings, Presidents and Prime Ministers in the world which are loaded with the army of the helpers and the workers. Besides it has also been noted that almost all of the serving members are supposed to be 100 per cent loyal and committed towards their mentors. It is certified by history that there were instances in ancient times when the whole staff of the Emperor was buried alive along with the King as to maintain loyalty and secrecy and to show the manumit and magnamity towards the Ruler for all times to come. As against this nothing of such type happened during the days of the Ruler of Islamic state. He had no pomp and show as mentioned above. There were hardly one or two persons to help him in his household work and to them also he did not consider as servants but loved them as the members of his family.

HIS WEALTH AND POSSESSIONS

As a matter of fact the Mighty Ruler of Islamic Confederation had no wealth and riches. When his father died he left behind five camels, a small number of goats, a she servant called Barakah Umm Aiman who later served him as his nursemaid. Despite being the most powerful rulers of his time he used to repair his own shoes, sew or mend his dress, avoid insects upon his clothes and used to do what ordinary men did in their houses. Milking the sheep and catering for himself were some of his normal jobs. When A'ishah, the wife of the Holy Ruler was asked what he did while he was in the home? She replied, "He would either be fulfilling the needs of his family members or serving them."[3] His living was very simple and his lifestyle resembled to that of ordinary human beings. A day before his death he had set all his slaves free, paid seven Dinars which he owned in charity and gave his weapons as present to Muslims and hence when night fell his beloved Empress A'ishah had to borrow some oil from her neighbour to light her oil-lamp. Even his armour was mortgaged as a security with a Jew for thirty Sa' (a cubic measure) of barley. When he died his august body was shrouded in three white Sahooli cotton cloth which had neither a head-cloth nor a casing. He was buried at the same place where he died in a room ten feet by ten feet. It is interesting to note that not only he was devoid of any wealth and possessions, his wives, children and relations too were living under dire necessities. His dearest daughter Fatima who was the Majestic Princess of an Exalted Highness of those times and whom he loved more than his life was living in odd conditions. She had no servants and no helpers and did all the household work herself. She used to grind grains on the millstone daily and her hands used to become blistered from working on the grinding stones. Since she had to wash the utensils herself and sweep the floor personally, her clothes became dirty from doing such odd jobs. Not only this, she had a mark on her neck from having to bring water from outside in a large leather bag. On one occasion when many servants and war booties in abundance came to the Ruler of Islam, Ali, the distinguished Court Advisor and the husband of Princess Fatima suggested her to go to her father and request him for one of the servants for her. She went but having found large people surrounding the Ruler, she could not muster courage and returned empty handed. Next day when the Exalted Steward of Islam came to her house he asked what she wanted to discuss. The Grand Princess kept quiet and Majestic Ali told the whole story. Thereupon, he did not say yes to her demand but told her to fear God and fulfill her duty to Allah. He advised her to continue to do her work and when she go to the bed at night, glorify Allah 33 times, praise Him the same number of times and exalt him 34 times. This will do her more good than the servant. The world knows that the Magnificent Princess did not utter a single word of complain or dissatisfaction but gladly and cheerfully accepted what was told to her.

RULER DECIDED TO LIVE LIKE ORDINARY PEOPLE

It is unthinkable and beyond imagination and perception of the intellectuals and the common men that the fire seldom lit in the house of the Ruler of Arabian Peninsula for days and he and his family had to depend upon dates and water and some milk of she camels which the kind Ansari neighbours used to send to him. It also happened that many times they did not eat evening meals and slept hungry. He hardly got his meal twice a day in the morning and evening with full stomach consisting of meat and bread for most of the time in his life. Likewise, he rarely ate bread with full stomach continuously for three days while he remained at Medina. He seldom touched roasted mutton and bread made up of white flour. His bread consisted mostly of barley. It occasionally happened that he ate even the dates of inferior quality with full stomach. Once he visited Umm Hani bint Abi Talib, his close relative when he was hungry and asked her to bring some food which he could eat. She told that she had only dried bread. He told her to bring that. She broke the bread in pieces, mixed water in it and poured some salt and gave it to him. He asked whether she had anything to eat with bread. She replied some vinegar. He asked her to bring which he poured over his food and ate thanking God by saying how good was vinegar with food.[4] He passed many nights in dark due to paucity of burning oil. One should note it very carefully that it was not because of his poverty or lack of resources. He was a mighty Ruler of the Islamic state in which he had one fifth share in every war booty. If he desired, he could live the life of Monarchs, Kings and Emperors but he willingly and deliberately remained under constrained conditions and never used the resources of the state for his personal use but distributed all his share among the destitute and the deserving people. He preferred the poverty ridden state of life because he knew that among his followers there would be millions of people who would not get their meals twice a day. He wanted to put before them his example so that they could accept their poverty as a blessing and Sunna of their leader rather than a curse. One should not forget that he could live a princely life even when he was not the Ruler but was struggling in Makkah. It is stated on the authority of Jabir b.'Abd Allah that Abu Jahal and some of the chiefs of Quraish contacted the Prophet and said, "If you have a desire for leadership, we are willing to announce you our leader, if you aspire for riches, we would collect for you an immense amount of wealth that will not only be sufficient for you but would also be enough even for your progenies; if you are moved by sexual impulses, you may choose ten beautiful virgins out of the whole tribe of Quraish." Holy Prophet replied that if they put Sun on his one palm and the Moon on the other even then he would not abandon his objective of spreading the message of Islam among people. Being a leader of whole mankind he preferred to live the life of a commoner despite being the mighty and gracious Ruler of one of the largest kingdoms of those days. In matters of eating, drinking, dressing and household matters he kept his original simplicity despite ascending to the apex of power and when he left for heavenly abode he did not leave gems, jewels, heaps of gold and silver, magnificent crown and the splendid throne, glamorous palaces and majestic mansion and retinue of servants and attendants but a mattress of dried palm leaves, a water-skin and an armour which too was mortgaged to a Jew.

THE EMPRESSES AND OTHER HELPERS OF THE RULER

It is irony of fate that Holy Prophet is sometimes criticized for marrying more than one wife when the fact is that being the Exalted Ruler of a mighty state he could marry as many women as he liked. Besides, plural marriages were a significant custom in those days and divorces too were very easy. However, he desisted from doing that. It is the fact of history that at his prime age of 25 years he married an elderly woman who was twenty years older than he. He came in contact with khadijah, a widow business woman when he carried her merchandize to Syria. She was so impressed by his honesty, sincerity and faithfully executing the whole task that she married her young agent at the age of 45. He remained devoted to her throughout 26 years of his life and did not forget her even after her death. The marriage gave him rank among the nobles of Makkah and provided him a strong supporter in his mission. He had sons and daughters with her but none of his sons survived save the daughters Zainab, Ruqaiya, Umm Kulthum and Fatima. After the death of his beloved wife Khadija, he married other women, all of whom were divorcees, except for A'ishah. Six of his wives were from the tribes of Quraish and five from different Arabian tribes and one was from the Coptic Christian in Egypt and she was the mother of his son Ibraheem. He married the women not for obsession of attaining worldly desires because most of them were either elderly or widows. He married them merely for political and social reasons as well as for 'Da'wa' that is; to spread the message of Islam among all sections and segments of the society and some of them he married to help them due to distress. He had to do it because he wanted to gain the loyalty of some nobles and tribes. He married some of the wives of his companions who had died while fighting in Jihad or while participating at Da'wa. Despite the fact that they were widows and older than him he married them to accommodate them and their dependents. He was just, loyal and sincere to all of them and never discriminated them but loved them with the core of his heart.

If we analyze his marriages to different women of various tribes and communities, we find that he married Sawdah bint Zam'a at the age of fifty who was the previous wife of As-Sakran bin 'Amr her paternal cousin and who was in great distress and had suffered immensely for the cause of Islam. A year later he married Aishah, the daughter of his most beloved friend Abu Bakr. She was the only virgin he married in his life and who later on proved to be the most learned women in Islamic Jurisprudence. The battles of Badr and Uhud had led to the martyrdom of several believers and there were helpless widows and the orphans. In order to support them Holy Prophet married Hafshah bint 'Umar bin Al-khattab in the third year of Hijra. Her ex-husband was khunais bin Hudafa but he was killed in the battle of Badr. Likewise, in the fourth year of Hijra he married Zainab bint Khuzaimah from Bani Hilal bin 'Amir bin Sasa'a, the widow of Abdullah bin Jahsh who was martyred at Uhud. Zainab had none to support her as her parents had discarded her as they were polytheists. She died two or three months after her marriage. He married Umm Salamah Hind bint Abi Omaiya the widow of Abu Salama who died due to the wounds suffered during the Battle of Uhud and who had left behind a pregnant wife and a daughter. She died in the fourth year of Hijra. His seventh wife was Zainab bint Jahsh who was from the family of Prophet's paternal cousin and who had been divorced by Zaid bin Haritha. Holy Prophet married Zainab bint Jahsh to his freed slave. The family of Zainab was willing to marry her to the Prophet but not to Zaid but Holy Prophet prevailed upon them. However, being unequal marriage, it could not survive for too long despite several conciliatory efforts of the Prophet. Since he was behind the agonies of Zainab, he had to marry her. He also married Zainab b. Jahsh to abolish the custom of the days of ignorance which prohibited a man from marrying the wife of his adopted son. Apart from marrying the widows and destitute from among the believers, he also married three widows from the enemy tribes. In the sixth year of Hijra, he married Juwairiyah bint Al-Harith. After accomplishing the covenant with Thabit bin Qais bin Shammasa' in the seventh year of Hijra he married Umm Habibah, the widow of Ubadullah bin Jahsh who had converted to Christianity and who had died in Abyssinia. Holy Prophet freed Safiyah bint Huyai bin Akhtab of children of Israel and married her as per her desire in the seventh year of Hijra. Lastly, he married Malmunah bint Al-Harith who was the daughter of Al-Harith and the sister of Umm Al-Fadi Lubabah bint Al-Harith in the seventh year of Hijra. Thus, Holy Prophet married eleven women, nine of whom survived after his death. The two wives with whom he did not consummate his marriage were from Bani Kilab and Kindah tribes. Thus the above facts reveal that at the fag end of his life when he became one of the biggest Rulers of Islamic Empire he married other women almost all of whom were widows or divorcees just to develop close contacts with various warring tribes and develop with them cordial relations. For instance, he married Umm Salamah who was from the influential tribe of Bani Makhzum—the clan of Abu Jahal and Khalid bin Al-Waleed. Waleed despite being a hardened opponent of Islam later on converted to the faith. Similarly, after the marriage of Umm Habibah, Abu Sufyan did not remain a hardened enemy. Likewise, his marriages to Aishah daughter of Abu Bakr, Hafshaw, the daughter of Umar developed among them close family relations. Not only this, he married his daughter Fatima to Ali bin Abi Talib and his two daughters Ruqayah and Umm Kulthum to Uthman with a view to have better contacts with the eminent tribes of those days. Over and above this, his wives helped him in spreading Islam among the womenfolk and they proved as ideals for women of Islam in the long run.

It is a fact that being the Ruler he was entitled to marry or keep as many concubines as he liked as per customs and practices among kings and Emperors those days. Polygamy was not only the established institution during Biblical and Talmudic times, the Mosaic Law also encouraged it. According to Encyclopedia Biblica, a Jew could marry as many as four wives and a king up to eighteen. The Rig veda and other religious books of Indians testify that during the Epic era the Kings and the Heroes could keep as many wives and concubines as they liked. Likewise, many spiritual leaders since time immemorial are believed to have more than one hundred wives. Polygamy was practised in Christianity during Middle Ages and it continued as late as seventeenth century. Emperor Taizong of Tang (599-649) was the second emperor of the Tang Dynasty of China. He was said to have had more than 3,000 concubines, although it has also been reported that during the Qing dynasty, the last imperial ruler of China, had around 20,000 concubines. In the Bible, 1 Kings 11:3 said that King Solomon had 700 wives and 300 concubines. Buddhist legends state that Ashoka kept a harem of around 500 women.

The above facts abundantly reveal that the Majestic Ruler of Islamic kingdom was never interested in marrying many wives or keeping several concubines. Those who have criticized him due to his marrying eleven wives had either not read his biography thoroughly or they were extremely biased persons. The world knows that during the period when he was at the peak of life and plural marriages was considered the general rule, he married only one wife though she was older than him and remained faithful till she remained alive. Behind plural marriages at the latter phase of his life were political, social, religious and legislative purposes. Besides, the facts also testify that he never discriminated between his wives due to outward differences and remained just and fair towards them. Once when the Mighty Ruler of Islam was sitting near 'A'ishah, one of his wives. She started telling the stories of eleven wives during Pre-Islamic days in much details consuming much time. The stories were very lengthy but he listened them attentively showing his positive inclination wherever it was necessary despite his most busy life. He did not show his boredom despite being tired and busy and convinced her that he understood the stories thoroughly and he was not lost elsewhere. Besides, in order to convince her that he was very attentive he compared himself with one of the two husbands of the eleventh wife named Umm Zar' whose first husband was very prosperous, compassionate and considerate but had divorced her and married another woman. Her second husband too was not bad but still she remembered the first one named Abu Zar. The Majestic Ruler of Islamic Kingdom told her that he was to her like Abu Zar' as Abu Zar' was to Umm Zar'.[5] Likewise, when Hafsha, the wife of the Ruler betrayed the confidentiality of a matter communicated to her by him, he did not retaliate. One day he visited her when she had a guest named Ash-Shifa' bint 'Abdullah, a female companion and a medical student who used to treat patients. He wanted to bring the attention of Hafsha to her mistake by approaching the issue indirectly so as to be gentle with her. He told Ash-Shifa, "Would you teach her the incantation of the ants, the way you taught her to write?" The famous incantation of ants was composed as: "the bride celebrates dyes, applies kohl and does everything else, except that she does not disobey her husband." The Holy Ruler wanted to indirectly teach Hafsha a lesson by repeating "...except that she does not disobey her husband."[6] He was indeed a just, polite, loving and a considerate husband. Thomas Carlyle says that "he was not a sensual man. We shall err widely if we consider this man as a common voluptuary, intent mainly on base enjoyments—nay on enjoyments of any kind."[7]

CONCLUSION

Has the humanity produced any Emperor amongst the series of world's greatest Emperors who despite being the exalted Ruler of one of the mightiest empires of his days lived in thatched cells? Can the living history cite any example of any Monarch who despite being the owner of one fifth of state exchequer distributed all of his wealth among the deserving and needy and went home empty handed and slept hungry along with his family members because there was nothing to eat? Have the world's historians read any biography of any mighty and gracious king whose domain was extended to far off areas covering many countries, cultures and civilizations but he lived a life stitching his own clothes and doing all the household chores by himself? Can the thinkers, philosophers, intellectuals and geniuses of the globe show any renowned Ruler who was respected by the greatest and mightiest men of his time due to his magnanimity and grace but when he left this world there was no oil in his house to light the lamp? Can all the encyclopedias of all the libraries of the world show us any instance of any splendid Leader who despite being crowned as the Chief of Arabian Peninsula had neither any pakka house, nor wore any crown nor sat on any throne, nor had any bodyguard but ruled his empire like an ordinary man? Has the mankind heard from any source that a Majestic Sovereign Power whose uncle's liver was chewed by his adversaries, his daughters were divorced by his enemies, he and his whole family and friends and relatives were brutally tortured by his dreaded foes forgave all of them unconditionally when he conquered them and when they were at his mercy? Have the Sun and Moon seen any individual since eternity ruling a significant part of the world whose private and public life were wide open before his subjects and whose all actions were just, transparent and equitable? Have the Stars and Galaxies watched any chief moving door to door in the dark of night merely to see whether any of his subjects was in trouble or had any grievance from his governing machinery? Have the angels and the jinn seen any just and impartial Ruler on the pages of history who ruled with absolute truth and justice and never showed any partiality and declared that he would cut the hand of everyone committing theft be she her dearest princess Fatima? Have the birds and trees seen any living being moving on any part of the world who despite being the mightiest King on earth was not only compassionate to human beings but was also kind to animals, insects, plants and trees? Have the winds and clouds seen any Mighty power controlling the major segment of the earth in whose rule neither any individual questioned his authority nor any revolt took place nor any of his companion aspired for any favour from him and nor his subjects felt any complaint? Has the earth ever given birth to any leader who not only governed his people with their consultations and for their benefits but also gave them a complete code of life from cradle to the grave?

Save the Ruler of Islam the accumulated experience of humanity from the treasuries of wisdom and knowledge cannot cite any case of any Emperor, Monarch, King or Ruler in the annals of history who did what the Ruler of the Islamic state did. It was he and only he who not only ruled his subjects with utmost care but also taught them the art of governance, strategies to fight the adversaries, protocols to receive the emissaries and the etiquettes of good living. He guided them to ponder over the secrets of nature and manifestations of natural phenomena and transformed them into civilized and enlightened beings. Those who were uncultured, uncivilized and unlettered became thinkers, philosophers, scientists, researchers, pioneers and geniuses. They discovered virgin territories, obtained expertise in the art of medicine and surgery and surpassed in the field of astronomy and religion. They established world-fame learning centers, renowned research centers, wonderful hospitals and comfortable shelter homes for wayfarers. They developed artisanship, improved communication net work, gave flip to industry and trade and vitalized agriculture and farming. They trained their horses, sharpened their weapons, raised armed battalions and rolled over Roman, Egyptian and Persian empires. They conquered Spain, captured Gibraltar and Malta, subjugated Constantine pole, subdued North Africa and reached as far as China and

Indonesia. They dented the medieval economic, political and social organizations, changed the ancient behaviour patterns of the people and impacted the world culture and civilization.

The world has seen that many great men came and built strong forts and fortresses, constructed marvelous mansions and palaces, raised splendid victory towers and marvels of their dignities but all of them faded in obscurity. Similarly many meaningful people emerged on the scene and erected the symbols and portents of their grace and glory, fabricated monuments and mausoleums of their ancestors, established cities and towns, founded dynasties and kingdoms and created wonders and miracles but ultimately found that their handmade were decayed and demolished over time at the hands of the vagaries of nature. Likewise, those nations who ruled the waves of the seas and those countries in whose kingdoms the sun never set or those people who had their supremacies in the skies saw that their memories withered away in no time for all times to come. However, those who prepared our minds for the acceptance of truth and justice, nurtured our hearts for love and compassion, guided us on the path of piety and peaceful co-existence and fashioned our conscience to hear the voice of reason and sanity are surviving till-date as the light houses of humanity.

Muhammad (PBUH), the Exalted Ruler was indeed one such influential man of history whose name, fame and contribution have been amply recorded in golden letters even after fourteen centuries of his departure from this world. Thousands of people young and old, men and women, Russians and Americans, Indians and Pakistanis, Indonesians and Malaysians, Arabs and Africans gather everyday to visit Masjid-e-Nabvi to seek his blessings. With weeping heart, tearful eyes and trembling hands they recite his praise profusely. Since they love the Ruler more than their dearest and nearest, they also cherish every inch of the sacred places where he performed his glorious activities while he was alive. Muslim heads of states and important dignitaries as well as business magnates, intellectuals, thinkers, philosophers, chiefs and leaders too aspire to have a glimpse of Medina.

Uncountable people across the world praise him daily in their five daily prayers and every Muslim looks at him for salvation at the time of the Day of Judgment. History testifies to this fact that he is the most cherished; most admired and most loved one in the world. No person in the universe ruled the hearts, minds and souls of the people so much since creation till date as the Holy Prophet and the Ruler of Islamic kingdom. Muslims throughout the world cannot hear anything adverse against him. Innumerable people are willing to die for him. They follow his Sunna (practices of the Holy Prophet) in their day to day life and follow the path charted by him. He is their master, guide, ideal, benefactor and saviour. Such distinction, recognition and honour have not been showered upon any man on earth save him.

The whole world admits that he was the greatest man as well as the most powerful, most outstanding and superlative personage who ever lived on this globe. He not only influenced the course of history but also shaped our lives and reformed the world. He was exclusively responsible for bringing revolution in the thought processes, deeds and perceptions of the multitude. According to Michael H. Hart, "he was the only man in history who was supremely successful on both the religious and secular levels." He invited the bewildered Arabs from the depth of polytheism to pure monotheism and taught them wisdom, imparted the art of decent living, refined their conducts and revolutionized their economic, political, social and cultural institutions. He is generally acknowledged as the Last Prophet of God but he was also the founder of Islamic Empire. He was not the Ruler who merely moved with the times but changed the contours of time since he was one who was too far ahead of his time. His genius and foresight profoundly influenced the subsequent history and diverted it towards the new path chartered by him which it might not otherwise have followed. He was far more original, far more innovative and far more devoted to his ideas and ideology but always believed in consultations and mutual consensus. He brought cultural renaissance during his reign and united the warring tribes of Arabia into a powerful and homogeneous force. Starting as a peer of a few followers he defeated Quraish, Jews, Bedouins and hostile Arab tribes by a series of victories and shattered the foundations of Byzantine, Persian and Egyptian Empires. He was exclusively responsible for all the conquests during his time and they could not have occurred without him. Likewise, it was the impact of his remarkable personality that Bedouins of Arabia inspired by his words carved out the largest empire that the world had yet seen. The Ruler of Islam was certainly a leader of immense military ability as he had embarked upon one of the most surprising victories in human history but that was merely one facet of his personality.

Basically he was one of the rarest men who single-handedly altered the course of history. His fame is not mainly due to winning all the battles that he fought but of great importance is the fact that the empire that he established during the shortest period of his life permanently altered the geographical, logistic, strategic and political structure of the contemporary world. His significance lies in the fact that while analyzing the influence of the Ruler of Islam on the world history one should keep this thing in mind that what he did for mankind and what he accomplished for his cause would surely and certainly never have been possible without him. The lands of Caesar, Cyrus and Pharaoh and other empires despite their territorial extent and duration could not stand before the onslaught of victories which he had unleashed during his ten years at Medina. No one would have expected that within forty years of his demise, most of the ancient world would be under the subjugation of an obscured tribe from Arabia.

More prominent was the benign character of his rule. He was a thoroughly admirable and a remarkably humane Ruler of his time. His career represents one of the major turning points in world history. From 3000 B.C. till his times many civilizations such as Sumerian, Acadian, Babylonian, Assyrian, Mesopotamian, Persian, Aryan, Chinese, etc. had dominated the world scene but his career brought that chapter of world history to end because from then onward the centre of the civilized world politically, economically, culturally and morally had shifted towards Medina, Makkah and the surrounding areas. He was exceptionally tolerant to others religions and customs and absolutely disinclined to the extreme cruelties, brutalities and injustices which characterized so many Kings, Emperors and Conquerors of those days. Babylonians and Assyrians, for instance, had massacred many thousand and had exiled whole people whose rebellion they feared. When Babylonians conquered Judea in 586 B.C., they deported much of the population to Babylonia. He never did this with his vanquished. The policy of assimilation and brotherhood that he instituted in his system was a major factor in the transformation of Islam into a great force. Arabia was an underdeveloped and entirely backward region, institution of serfdom was flourishing in every town, illiteracy was showing its ugly head, poverty, ignorance and superstition were rampant and literature and science were despised but when he died in 632 A.D., he had not only transformed the whole economic, social, cultural and religious milieu of Arabs but made them pioneers in the field of science, arts, humanities, geography and law. It is the considered opinion of all the sensible people from various segments of different societies across the world that such a distinguished, unique and famous man has neither been born on any part of the earth since creation nor shall be born till destruction of the universe. He shall be guiding mankind as a torch bearer on the path of peace, progress, harmony and salvation till the days and nights remain in operation and till the Sun and Moon shine on the firmament.

Finally, we can conclude by the famous poem of Allama Iqbal on Prophet Muhammad (PBUH):

> He slept on a mat of rushes,
> But the crown of Chosroes lay beneath the feet of his followers;
>
> He chose the nightly solitude of Mount Hira,
> And founded a nation, law and government;
>
> He passed his nights with sleepless eyes,
> That his Millet might sleep on Chosroes throne

In the hour of battle, iron was melted by the flash of his sword.

At prayer time, tears fell like drops of rain from his eyes.
In his prayer for Divine help, his Amen' was a sword,
Which extirpated the lineage of kings.

He inaugurated a new Order in the world,
He brought the empires old to an end:

In his sight the high and the low were one,
He sat with the slave at table one;

He burnt clear the distinctions of birth and clan.
His fire consumed all this trash and bran.

NOTES

1. Abdul Hameed Siddiqui, op. cit., p. 143.
2. Dr. Muhammad Al-Afreefi, op. cit., p. 452.
3. *Ibid.*, p. 423.
4. *Ibid.*, p. 298.
5. *Ibid.*, pp. 382-86.
6. *Ibid.*, 392.
7. Abdurrahman, op. cit., p. 60.